OTHER BOOKS BY CAROL WESTON

For Girls Only:
Wise Words, Good Advice

Girltalk:
All the Stuff Your Sister Never Told You

Private and Personal:
Questions and Answers for Girls Only

The Diary of Melanie Martin
or How I Survived Matt the Brat,
Michelangelo, and the Leaning Tower of Pizza

Melanie Martin Goes Dutch
The Private Diary of My Almost Bummer Summer
with Cecily, Matt the Brat, and Vincent van Go Go Go

From Here to Maternity:
Confessions of a First-Time Mother

How to Honeymoon

Girltalk About Guys

+for teens oNLY

quotes, & notes, advice you can use

caroL weston

HarperTrophy®

An Imprint of HarperCollins*Publishers*

This book is dedicated to

me

because I've already dedicated books to

my husband, daughters, parents, brothers,

nephews, and niece

and because this one's about

feeling good about yourself.

Harper Trophy® is a registered trademark of HarperCollins Publishers Inc.

For Teens Only:
Quotes, Notes, and Advice You Can Use
Copyright © 2003 by Carol Weston
Printed in the United States of America. For information address
HarperCollins Children's Books, a division of HarperCollins Publishers,
1350 Avenue of the Americas, New York, NY 10019.

Library of Congress Cataloging-in-Publication Data
Weston, Carol.
For teens only : quotes, notes, and advice you can use / Carol Weston. — 1st Harper Trophy ed.
    p.   cm.
    ISBN 0-06-000214-X (pbk.)
    1. Teenagers—Life skills guides. 2. Teenagers—Conduct of life. 3. Conduct of life—Quotations,
maxims, etc. I. Title.
HQ796 .W4714 2003   2002006381
646.7′00835—dc21   CIP
                                                                                        AC

Typography by Karin Paprocki
❖
First Harper Trophy edition, 2003
Visit us on the World Wide Web!
www.harperteen.com

contents

First Lines   1

Mind   7

Body   31

Friends   63

Relationships   97

School   141

Family   175

Work   203

End Quotes   229

Index   237

Acknowledgments   247

mindbodyfriendsrelationshipsschoolfamilyworkquote

mindbodyfriendsrelationshipsschoolfamilyworkquotesadvice

FIRST LINES

mindbodyfriendsrelationshipsschoo

I always do the first lines well,

but I have trouble doing the others.
MOLIÈRE

It isn't where you come from,

it's where you're going that counts.
—ELLA FITZGERALD

We're lost but we're making good time.
—YOGI BERRA

Life is so precious. Please, please, let's love one another.
—JULIA ROBERTS

Only dumb people try to impress smart people.

Smart people just do what they do.
—CHRIS ROCK

The great thing to learn about life is, first,

not to do what you don't want to do, and second,

to do what you do want to do.
—MARGARET ANDERSON

What is the meaning of life? To be happy and useful.
—THE DALAI LAMA

The future depends entirely on what each of us does every day.
—GLORIA STEINEM

The best things in life aren't things.
—anonymous

All the darkness of the world cannot
extinguish the light of a single candle.
—Saint Francis of Assisi

The hilltop hour would not be half so wonderful if
there were no dark valleys to traverse.
—Helen Keller

Knowledge comes but wisdom lingers.
—Alfred, Lord Tennyson

Many receive advice. Only the wise profit from it.

—PUBLIUS SYRUS

W elcome to this book. I enjoyed writing it and I hope you enjoy reading it. If you need a quote for your paper or yearbook or speech, *For Teens Only* has 580. If you need advice or insights or encouragement, it's got that, too.

Ralph Waldo Emerson said, "I hate quotations. Tell me what you know."

What I know is that I love quotations, always have. Shakespeare, Maya Angelou, Mark Twain, Gwyneth Paltrow, Groucho Marx, Whoopi Goldberg, Buddha, and Homer Simpson have all said things that may surprise you, inspire you, make you laugh, or make you think. My words on Mind, Body, Friends, Relationships, School, Family, and Work can provide practical wisdom, too.

Do any of us have all the answers? No.

But this book, this collection of voices, can shine some light on the road ahead as you find your own voice, your own answers, your own wisdom.

On your mark, get set, go!

MIND

bodyfriendsrelationshipsschoolfamilyworkquotesadvice

You are a marvel. You are unique.
You may become a Shakespeare, a Michelangelo,
a Beethoven. You have the capacity for anything.
—PABLO CASALS

In college I had a thing for guys with accents. Some of my friends melted over guys who were athletic or musical or funny. My weakness was men who could say my name in a way I'd never heard before.

I ended up marrying a wonderful guy from Columbus, Ohio, but on the way to the altar I spent several romantic years with Juan, a poet from Madrid. I loved it when he used the flattering phrase *Eres una maravilla*—"You are a marvel." Juan said it a lot. Maybe cellist Pablo Casals did, too. Maybe many Spaniards do.

I'm starting this book by saying it to you: *Eres una maravilla.*

You are a marvel. You are amazing. You are unique. You are the only you in the whole wide world. You have the potential to do great things and to be happy—whether or not you feel this way right now.

We all have moments of self-doubt (and reasons to doubt ourselves). But we also have reasons to celebrate ourselves. To feel proud. Powerful. Inspired.

Think about what you have going for you. Dare to take stock of your best qualities.

Pretty impressive, right?

You have what it takes.

*To be nobody-but-yourself in a world that is doing
its best night and day to make you everybody else means
to fight the hardest battle that any human being
can fight; and never stop fighting.*

—E. E. CUMMINGS

Seems like it would be easy to be true to yourself. You're you and that's that.

Well, it turns out it can be tricky to figure out how to fit in without blurring in. How to be part of a group but still be your own person. How to feel accepted without having to downplay your differences or pretend to care about things you don't care about. How to say yes when you want to say yes, and no when you want to say no.

In some schools, everyone wears the same clothes, admires the same people, likes the same music, movies, and TV shows, and lusts after the same chosen few. Is your school like that?

It's comfortable to be one of the crowd. But it also feels good to be one of a kind.

"The privilege of a lifetime is being who you are," wrote Joseph Campbell.

"Always be a first-rate version of yourself instead of a second-rate version of somebody else," said Judy Garland, who played Dorothy in *The Wizard of Oz.*

Stay aware of what is special about you. Keep track of the you that only you know.

Hear the crowd, but listen to yourself, because you just may want to blaze your own trail.

If you won't be you . . . who will?

I think there's something idiotic about the self,

that every day you have to get up and be the same person. . . .

It can be somewhat infuriating to wake up and find that one

has the same characteristics that one had when

one went to bed the night before.

—Wallace Shawn

Some people think we're evolving all the time. When Lewis Carroll's Caterpillar asks Alice in Wonderland, "Who are *you?*" she answers quite honestly: "I—I hardly know, Sir, just at present—at least, I know who I *was* when I got up this morning, but I think I must have changed several times since then."

Other people think it's impossible to change—that the self is a given. "If God had wanted me otherwise, he would have created me otherwise," said German writer Johann Wolfgang von Goethe.

Who are you and who are you becoming? To find out, notice which people you are drawn to. What subjects do you like best? What movies? What music? What books? What sports? Pay attention to what upsets you, what calms you, and what makes you laugh. Think about what you love to talk about with friends, and what they talk about with you. When you meet new people, what strikes them about you? What surprises them later, when they know you better? Are you easygoing? Conscientious? Are you a leader? A risk-taker?

"For years you've felt only half-done inside, cobbled together by paper clips, held intact by gum wads and school paste," wrote author Mary Karr. "But something solid is starting to assemble inside you. You say, I am my same self. That's not nothing, is it?"

What makes you you?

Being yourself gets easier and easier.

If you're not happy with yourself, then yeah,
you need to make some changes. But if other people
aren't happy with you, but you are? Guess what?
You're way ahead of the game.
—Freddie Prinze Jr.

"Say someone offered you a new personality, would you take it? Say somebody said to you, *I will permanently rewire your mental hardware in whatever way you want.* Would you pay to have that done?" asked a character in Jonathan Franzen's novel *The Corrections.*

There might be a few things you'd tweak, but you wouldn't get yourself overhauled, would you? You wouldn't want to mess with your essence, right?

What are the qualities about you that you like best? Are you thoughtful? Smart? Funny? Generous? Patient? Athletic? Attractive?

Don't just yearn to be more athletic or attractive. Value who you are! Then, sure, work at becoming more thoughtful or patient—or even more athletic or attractive.

My friend Roger was just twenty-one when his dad died. He remembers his father's last words to him: "Be the best Roger you can be." Much better advice than just "Be yourself" or "Do your best." His father pushed him to take himself to the next level.

Can you do that? Can you be the best <u>your name here</u> you can be?

Nobody is perfect, and you're already pretty wonderful. But as actress Katharine Hepburn said, "If you want to change, you're the one who has got to change. It's as simple as that, isn't it?"

Be a work-in-progress and keep progressing.

Growing up, I didn't excel at anything. I was very average and mediocre. I didn't have anything to claim for myself.

—Julia Roberts

"Adolescence hit me like a wallop," said the Oscar-winning actress. Adolescence? Many adults might borrow Charles Dickens's line: "It was the best of times, it was the worst of times."

None of us starts out knowing what our strong suits are. In school, it wasn't clear that Julia Roberts was movie star material. (And while I liked English, I was far too upset about having braces but not having breasts to picture myself as a future author, let alone advice giver.)

Some of your classmates may invent or create or achieve something very cool. From my high school there's a famous actor; a musician who went platinum; a Pulitzer Prize–winning journalist. From your school, there may be . . . you!

You are, after all, still discovering and developing your talents. You are full of promise, whether you know it or not. Your options are wide open, and you have years and years to realize your dreams.

Even if you do not yet have an obvious talent or mapped-out master plan, you have it in you to do amazing things, small or large, private or public. And you get to define "amazing" any way you want.

Time is on your side.

Some people think of the glass as half full.
Some people think of the glass as half empty.
I think of the glass as too big.
—george carlin

Attitude makes all the difference.

Woody Allen said, "I'm not confident. I would say I've lived my life braced for a blow."

John Lennon, on the other hand, said, "When I was a Beatle, I thought we were the best group in the world—and it was just a matter of time before everyone else caught on."

You can't totally control whether you're a pessimist or an optimist, cowering or cocky. But you can work on a winning attitude. You can get in the habit of telling yourself that you're doing fine, you've succeeded in the past, you have people who are rooting for you. You can pump yourself up rather than tear yourself down. (Example: "Yay me! I got some exercise!" not "Just twenty minutes on the treadmill—how pathetic!")

"We either make ourselves miserable, or we make ourselves strong. The amount of work is the same," said writer Carlos Castaneda.

It can be easy to sink into loser-itis and start comparing yourself unfavorably to others, but it's self-defeating and can become a bad habit. "Nobody holds a good opinion of a man who holds a low opinion of himself," said novelist Anthony Trollope.

So be as supportive of yourself as you are (or should be!) of your friends. It's not all about getting the grand prize anyway. It's about enjoying the small delights along the way.

Don't fear failure. Assume success.

You will do foolish things, but do them with enthusiasm.

—colette

A re you enthusiastic!?

"Enthusiasm is the most important thing in life," said Tennessee Williams.

I married Robert because of his enthusiasm. (I also found him kinda cute.) Rob loves cooking and eating out. He loves theater, loves volleyball, loves baseball, loves jazz, loves classical music, loves parties, loves travel, loves foreign movies, loves New York. He even loves me!

All that love is fun. And fun is good—and contagious in the best way.

"I have found that if you love life, life will love you back," said musician Arthur Rubinstein.

If you can find the positive in whatever you're up to, people will ask you to more parties, movies, concerts, and ball games. It's the opposite of a vicious cycle—it's a vibrant cycle!

If, however, you're usually down, and people know that if they call, they'll get an earful, they'll call less often, and you'll start living life less.

I'm not saying to pretend everything is great 24/7. It's okay to communicate your highs and lows. But if you're finding it hard to be revved up, try to be interesting or helpful or a good listener.

Put things on your calendar that you can look forward to. As author Maya Angelou advised, "You must laugh at least as much as you cry, just for balance."

Having fun counts.

Do human beings ever realize life while they live—

every, every minute?

—thornton wilder's emily webb

I t is hard to appreciate every, every minute. (And okay, some minutes do sort of stink.) But are you at least trying to appreciate life as you live it?

Instead of mumbling that you were hoping for pizza as your mom serves up chicken, try to be grateful for the dinner before you. Is the table conversation lame? Liven it up with a tidbit from school, or ask someone about his day, or past, or something he's looking forward to.

In *Our Town,* young Emily dies, then tells the other dead people in the graveyard that she wants to go visit Earth for a day. They say it's a lousy idea, but back Emily goes—and then she can hardly bear what she finds. It's her twelfth birthday, yet her family is so preoccupied with getting things done that they scarcely even see or talk to one another.

We're all guilty of taking things for granted and moving too fast. Wilder's point is that we should slow down and soak up the here and now. Talk to your family members—not just the person on your cell phone or computer screen. Connect with your friends and family and self.

Here's a Sanskrit poem: "Each today, well-lived, makes yesterday a dream of happiness and tomorrow a vision of hope. Look, therefore, to this one day, for it and it alone is life."

And here's what Japanese birth control pioneer, Shidzue Kato, said on her one hundredth birthday: "I stay positive by appreciating ten things a day."

Today is a gift. Enjoy the present.

Spend the afternoon. You can't take it with you.

—annie Dillard

C hildhood always ends.

Child star Shirley Temple lost her innocence abruptly. "I stopped believing in Santa Claus when I was six. Mother took me to see him in a department store and he asked for my autograph."

If some of your childhood is left, relish it! Enjoy being a teen rather than rushing headlong into adulthood with all its responsibilities.

You'll get there soon enough, believe me.

"Time happens," said playwright Edward Albee.

Take a look at where you are in your life and get into being there, whether you're twelve or seventeen, younger or older.

"It is so easy to waste our lives: our days, our hours, our minutes," said Anna Quindlen. "It is so easy to exist instead of to live."

Your mission, if you choose to accept it, is not just to exist, but to live.

Many children want to be teens, and many teens want to be adults. But many adults wish they could relive their youth!

"For years, I wanted to be older," mused Canadian novelist Margaret Atwood. "And now I am."

"What a wonderful life I've had!" said French writer Colette. "I only wish I'd realized it sooner."

Don't rush things. Relish them.

The time you enjoy wasting is not wasted time.

—Lawrence J. Peter

S trive for balance: Get things done—and have some fun.

If you need to hit the books harder, do so; if you need to let yourself out of the library, come on out.

When you're little, your parents manage time for you.

Now you're learning not just science, math, history, and English, but how to budget your time. How to fill your own afternoons and evenings and weekends.

That's a biggie.

"How we spend our days is, of course, how we spend our lives," said writer Annie Dillard.

I spend a lot of my day staring at a computer screen and tapping at a keyboard. But I also make sure to get a little sunshine, and I try to get to the gym, or a movie, museum, or friend's home when possible. I meet my deadlines, but I also say yes to diversions. And if that sometimes means playing poker or watching reruns of *Friends* with friends, that's not wasted time. That's time well-spent.

Work and play—both.

Learning to say no is probably the most difficult thing
I've ever had to do. And I highly recommend it.

ANN RICHARDS

Take it from the former governor of Texas: Learn to say no. Saying no to someone else often means saying yes to yourself. And as Bart Simpson put it: "Weaseling out of things is important to learn. It's what separates us from the animals—except the weasel."

I'm all for after-school activities. But don't overextend yourself. Don't say, "Count me in," if the demands will feel like a burden instead of a pleasure. "Our life is frittered away by detail," wrote Henry David Thoreau. "Simplify, simplify."

There are many things you have to do—for your parents, teachers, bosses, and self. But other things are optional. So notice when you're focused or enjoying yourself as opposed to when you're yawning at a meeting or channel-surfing or doing favors for nonfriends. If you're putting hours into something without getting much in return, be more protective of your time.

When I started middle school, I sometimes enlisted my parents' help when I needed to say no. I'd say, "Am I free to babysit?" while holding the phone and shaking my head. That was their cue to say, "Sorry, we have plans." Later, I got better at speaking for myself!

Try to figure out what people, activities, and goals matter most, and use your time accordingly.

Life is long and you can squeeze in an awful lot. But you can't sample every single item on the smorgasbord without getting a stomachache. Start deciding what belongs on your plate—and what doesn't.

Do what is important—important to do and important to you.

Oh my Lord I am absolutely so busy I don't know how
I can possibly get everything done.
—KaY tHOMPSON'S ELOISE

E loise, the precocious child who lives at the Plaza, stays busy busy busy making mischief mischief mischief.

We're all busy. Girls, guys, students, teachers, parents, mischief makers, world leaders, wildebeests, squirrels, ants, bees, even guppies.

Maybe not cats. Cats are mellow. Cats live to nap.

Assuming you are not a cat, you probably have more things to do than time to do them.

Joyce Carol Oates, the prolific author with the terrific middle name, said, "Most of the time I do nothing, and the fact of time passing so relentlessly is a source of anguish to me."

No matter how anguished you become, no one is ever going to award you a twenty-fifth hour. So set priorities. It may help to list what you want to do, short term and long term, for work and for pleasure. Then figure out what needs to be done first, and do it.

Fortunately, if you do prioritize, cut corners when necessary, and chip away at big projects, you can do what you need to do *and* what you want to do. Maybe not on any given single day, but in the Big Picture.

Just as Joyce Carol Oates keeps cranking out books, and Eloise keeps pouring water down mail chutes, you can find a way to do what matters to you.

Start with what matters most.

Four be the things I'd be better without:
Love, curiosity, freckles, and doubt.

I *like* love, curiosity, and freckles, but doubt can indeed be a big drag. It'd be so much tidier if everything were black and white, right or wrong.

But noooooooooo. Life has to be complicated.

"Doubt is not a pleasant condition, but certainty is absurd," wrote Voltaire.

No doubt about it: Doubt can make you feel uncomfortable or confused. But it's better to keep asking questions than to assume something is right. It's also better to question yourself than to assume the way you've always done something is the only way to do it.

To doubt is normal. Many brides and grooms admit to wedding day collywobbles, and all of us have smaller doubts even on no-big-deal days.

If you're polling all your friends about something rather than just doing it, this may mean you're not 100 percent committed to your plan.

Are you in doubt because you're a very deliberate person who weighs all situations carefully, or because this situation is worth serious reexamination?

List the pros and cons of saying yes or no before taking action. And seek advice from someone you trust.

But always consult yourself, too. As Jennifer Lopez said, "I believe in going with your gut instincts. When you go against them is when you go wrong."

Your brain and your gut make a great team.

21

Courage is being scared to death . . .

and saddling up anyway.

—JOHN WAYNE

"He who fears he will suffer already suffers from his fear," said Michel de Montaigne.

"To the timid and hesitating, everything is impossible because it seems so," said Sir Walter Scott.

"Life shrinks or expands in proportion to one's courage," wrote Anaïs Nin.

Lots of quotes, one message: Be brave.

Does this mean you should be reckless? No. "It is better to be a coward for a minute than dead for the rest of your life," counsels an Irish proverb.

But do find the courage to get out of your room—to help others and help yourself. Even in school, you can probably be more courageous. Are you quiet because you're afraid of sounding too smart or not smart enough? Jump in! Do you hang out with the exact same people day after day because you're reluctant to say hi to someone new? Smile at a stranger! Are you afraid to make mistakes? Make some mistakes!

"If you don't fail now and again, it's a sign that you're playing it safe," said Woody Allen.

"If you're going to fail, fail big, and take chances," said Denzel Washington, who succeeded at winning the Academy Award for Best Actor.

Keep challenging yourself and taking reasonable risks—ones that won't hurt you or anyone else.

Rise to the challenge.

One man with courage makes a majority.

—andrew Jackson

There are 6 billion people in the world, and each day, the overwhelming majority of them go about their business without much trouble. My hope is that our worries can always be little ones—worries of the Will-the-test-be-hard? and Will-we-win-the-game? variety.

But every so often, something can happen that scares people. Something terrible like an earthquake, or a school shooting, or an act of terrorism. Even then, a particular person's individual risk of harm is usually miniscule.

Should we be prepared for a crisis? Sure. Take CPR or tae kwon do. Learn the Heimlich maneuver. Stage a family fire drill. Stash flashlights, pills, candles, bottles of water, and cans of tuna in the pantry.

Thinking ahead, just in case, is sensible.

Hunkering down forever in fear is not.

And staying brave in the face of actual danger? That's heroism.

"I'm on the plane that's been hijacked," Thomas Burnett Jr. said on the phone to his wife on September 11, 2001. "There's three of us who are going to do something about it." Two planes had just struck and demolished the World Trade Center buildings, and a third had flown into the Pentagon. Thanks, probably, to Burnett and others, United Flight 93 crashed into a Pennsylvania field rather than a building full of innocent people. Like so many courageous firefighters and police officers, Burnett saved lives while losing his own.

"The world understands that whilst, of course, there are dangers in action," said British Prime Minister Tony Blair, "the dangers of inaction are far far greater."

Get to know your inner hero.

A sheltered life can be a daring life as well,

for all serious daring starts from within.

—eudora welty

Sometimes courage is public. Other times, it is private.

Are you courageous? Can you take control of your life rather than bob along wherever the current takes you? Can you figure out who you are and what you want? Can you think hard before going out with the first person who asks or accepting the first job that comes your way?

"Never let anyone else decide who you are," said comedian Caroline Rhea—whose mother always said it to her.

Keep figuring out who you are, and figure out, too, what you care about enough to work for—possibly even fight for.

"If we don't stand for something, we may fall for anything," cautioned African American leader Malcolm X.

"Each time a man stands up for an idea or acts to improve the lot of others, or strikes out against injustice," said Robert F. Kennedy, "he sends forth a tiny ripple of hope, and those ripples build a current that can sweep down the mightiest walls of oppression and resistance."

You don't yet know what you stand for? That's okay. These are the years for finding out. Your parents are Republican and your best friend is a Democrat? Read the paper and start forming your own opinions.

Search for your values.

24

The time is always right to do what is right.
—martin Luther King Jr.

Working to help others helps you, too. Not only because it puffs up your job résumé or college application, but because it feels good to be unselfish, to be of service.

"Good and kind people outnumber all others by thousands to one," wrote scientist Stephen Jay Gould. Find the kindest part of yourself and put it to use in big or little, visible or invisible, ways. Raise money for a cause; teach kids to read; be a Secret Santa; play music at a senior citizen center. Does your school have a community service bulletin board? Volunteer to clean a park, serve at a soup kitchen, or do peer counseling. Is there something that bugs you about the way your school works? Come up with a project to solve it.

In high school, I spent Saturday mornings in a swimming pool with children with disabilities. In college, I spent Tuesday evenings at a hospital's pediatric ward. You could, too. Helping others lifts spirits— theirs and yours.

Reach out to your own older relatives or discouraged friends. Sometimes just a smile or thank-you or two-second e-mail that says, "Thinking of you," or "Hang in there," or "Feel better" can make some-one else's day.

"What one does is what counts and not what one had the intention of doing," said Pablo Picasso. So don't say, "How was the audition? I meant to call." Or "I meant to visit you in the hospital," or "I was going to write my senator."

Call. Visit. Follow through. Do your part. Practice being a good person.

It feels good to do good.

No matter how big a nation is, it is no stronger than its
weakest people, and as long as you keep a person down,
some part of you has to be down there to hold him down,
so it means you cannot soar as you might otherwise.
—marian anderson

C an we all agree that racism and sexism and intolerance are hurtful, unfair, and stupid? Do you live in an area where everybody looks the same? I live in New York, a city that prides itself on *not* being homogeneous. Living here, you quickly realize that you can't presume to understand someone based on skin color (or gender or nationality or religion or sexual orientation or weight or hair).

Greek philospher Heraclitus wrote, "Dogs bark at a person whom they do not know." Get to know people—individuals and cultures.

John F. Kennedy warned against having "the comfort of opinion without the discomfort of thought." Think, always think.

There's no such thing as good people or bad people anyway. "If only it were so simple!" wrote Russian Nobel Prize winner Aleksandr Solzhenitsyn. "But the line dividing good and evil cuts through the heart of every human being."

Actor Edward James Olmos said, "There's only one race, and that's the human race. Period."

If you are not closeminded, but your relatives are, you may not be able to change them—but more power to you for seeing with your own eyes. As Gloria Steinem said, "The first problem for many of us is not to learn but to unlearn."

While I'm talking tolerance, why is the goal for us to tolerate one another? Why not *respect* one another? Why not celebrate our differences?

A mind is a terrible thing to close.

H ave you ever been the victim of an "-ism"? If so, your challenge is to
develop your strengths despite this and without becoming bitter.

Tony Award–winning playwright Tony Kushner wrote *Angels in America,* which is about the experience of being gay in the age of AIDS. Kushner knew that just complaining or going into victim-mode would do no good, whereas writing a great play could do lots of good—for himself and for theatergoers.

If you've been unjustly passed over or sneered at or interrogated, you are not alone, but that doesn't make things easier. It stinks to feel judged—let alone *pre*judged. My hope is that you can rise above the small-minded and shortsighted, focus on what's cool about being you, find your footing, then go on to excel in every way possible.

"Sometimes I feel discriminated against," said Zora Neale Hurston, "but it does not make me angry. It merely astonishes me. How can any deny themselves the pleasure of my company?"

"People don't even know when they're being racist," said Academy Award–winning actress Halle Berry, who added that her "mission" is "to make a way out of no way."

Can you turn things to your advantage? Some schools actively seek diversity. Why not apply to that long-shot private school or college? Find out about scholarships, too. And someday, when you take your place in the world, see how you can help others—or help change the system.

Be unstoppable.

There are three things I've learned never to discuss with people:
religion, politics, and the Great Pumpkin.

—LINUS IN *Peanuts,* BY CHARLES SCHULZ

'm with Linus, so you won't find much in this book on religion, politics, or the Great Pumpkin.

Some people can converse civilly about religious beliefs and political leanings. Others can't. And no matter how much you argue with them, very few people switch teams.

The Dalai Lama said, "My religion is simple. My religion is kindness."

Author Louis L'Amour said, "To disbelieve is easy; to scoff is simple; to have faith is harder."

It would be ideal if we could all just respect one another's right to pray or not pray, lean right or lean left. It would be ideal if no one scoffed—let alone threw grenades.

"Peace," said former president Benito Juárez of Mexico, "is respect for the rights of others."

Since hate and distrust can be as infectious as love and tolerance, try to be respectful and informed. Learn about different religions and governments. Keep up with world events. Find out not which *celebrities* are fighting but which *countries* are fighting.

"Let us not look back in anger or forward in fear but around in awareness," said writer James Thurber.

You never want to be a fanatic. But you always want to know where you stand.

There are no easy answers, but keep asking questions.

Our collective efforts to conserve can
actually make a difference.

—Bar·br·a Sor·eis·and

"**N**ever lose your zeal for building a better world," said educator Mary McLeod Bethune.

A quick reminder to turn off the lights when you leave a room, turn off the water while you're brushing your teeth, open the window instead of cranking the air conditioner, and use what you need and no more.

We Americans drive our fuel-guzzling megacars to all-you-can-eat restaurants where we fill our plates to the rim, then throw out enough food to feed hungry families.

Maybe your family seems to have unlimited resources and can afford to be wasteful. But our planet is crowded; its resources are limited.

So put on a sweater instead of pushing the heat to 72 degrees. Take two ketchup packets instead of grabbing five and discarding three. Recycle clothes, magazines, and kids' toys instead of throwing them away. Use a sponge instead of paper towels. Buy products in biodegradable boxes instead of plastic containers. And consider joining or forming an environmental awareness club at your school.

If you and I and everyone else tries to be less wasteful, the world will be better off. And the world is our home.

Mother Earth takes care of you; take care of her.

There must be more to life than having everything.

—maurice sendak

More, more, more still won't be enough if you live to shop or to own the latest clothes, shoes, gadgets, music, or cars.

For some, the pleasure of owning something new is immediately followed by a craving for something else or something newer. Happiness becomes elusive—always one purchase away.

When you watch TV, read a magazine, or pick up your mail, you are bombarded with commercials, ads, and catalogs trying to separate you from your money.

How many products do we even need? Soap, yes. Shampoo, yes. Deodorant, yes. Other creams, lotions, gels? Not really. "Everybody gets so much information all day long that they lose their common sense," said writer Gertrude Stein.

Keep your guard up. Corporations want you to want things. Materialism and consumerism keep the economy going; so do those who shop till they drop.

But I'm looking out for you, not the national debt.

People who have more stuff aren't automatically happier anyway. They just have more stuff.

Starry nights, long walks, blowing bubbles, telling stories, passing notes, playing ball, laughing, hugging, friendship, and love are all free— and priceless.

Appreciate what you already have.

BODY

The first wealth is health.

—raLPH WaLDO emerson

W hen you were a kid, your parents bathed you, dressed you, combed your hair, took you to the park, and fed you three meals a day, one spoonful of messy mush at a time. They even potty-trained you—but let's not go there.

Now that you're older, things are more dignified. You're in charge of your body—thank heavens. You could drink nothing but Coke, eat nothing but Fritos, and shower every other Friday. But not only would you become malnourished, you'd start to reek.

This chapter is about taking care of your body, looking good, feeling good, and accepting the physical changes you are (or are not) going through.

The main thing is not what you look like or if you've hit puberty. It's that your body *works*. That it walks and runs and eats and rests.

"If anything is sacred," Walt Whitman said, "the body is sacred."

Try to be healthy and stay healthy.

Take care of yourself.

Be not afraid of growing slowly,
be afraid only of standing still.
—CHINESE PROVERB

B elieve me, you're *not* standing still. You are changing every day at your own rate. It's happening. It's why your clothes keep shrinking and your aunt keeps saying, "I can't believe how much you've grown!"

Some kids develop early, some late. But everyone gets there. Puberty hasn't skipped anybody yet.

Right now you may wish you weren't ahead of or behind your classmates. You may feel impatient or out of sync with friends. But in a few short years, everybody will have developed, your body will feel like your own again, and these anxieties will be a distant memory.

For now, your body is going to do what it's going to do, and there's no way to slow things down or speed things up. No way to turn back the clock if you're an early bloomer, or rush Mother Nature if you're a late bloomer.

You can't change your body's timetable.

You *can* decide to stop worrying about it.

So if your body seems to be changing unpredictably, relax, it won't keep up this pace. And if your body isn't budging? As Jane Fonda pointed out, "It doesn't matter if you're a late bloomer as long as you don't miss the flower show."

Normal? Yes.

*There's no need for me to look in the mirror because
it's someone else's job to make sure I look like I should.*

—JULIA ROBERTS

M ust be nice to be a superstar.

What about the rest of us?

Go wild. Check yourself out from time to time. Don't automatically groan or gloat. Just make sure your hair isn't sticking up and there's no corn between your teeth.

Author Jean Kerr wrote,

> *Mirror, mirror, on the wall,*
> *I don't want to hear*
> *One word out of you.*

Yet sometimes a mirror's murmur can be helpful. As fashion editor Diana Vreeland said, "I loathe narcissism, but I approve of vanity."

Should you do what you can to look good? Sure—especially if you enjoy taking care of your appearance. But don't get so high-maintenance and preoccupied that you'd never leave home unless your hair were meticulously gelled or blow dried.

After all, while it's good to look good, it's better to feel good about how you look.

A little vanity goes a long way.

I was so ugly, the doctor slapped my mother!
—Henny Youngman

ome people see the world through rose-colored glasses. Some see it through ugly-colored glasses.

When you look in the mirror, do you ever see a pimple instead of a person? A cow instead of a human? Do you keep hoping for a different reflection?

If so, give yourself a break! If you were your best friend, you'd think you looked perfectly fine, right? So befriend yourself!

Musician Alicia Keys said, "You have to accept who you are—and that is beautiful." Or handsome!

When you look around, you don't zero in on other people's blemishes, facial hair, or whether their weight fluctuates slightly in either direction, do you? (Please tell me you're not that shallow!) Even when you do halfway notice that someone has a pimple, you don't fixate on it, right? You don't think less of the person.

You see your classmates and neighbors as Whole People, not as collections of flaws and failings. And that's how they see you. They aren't judging your skin or silhouette. They're appreciating you as is.

Treat yourself with the same respect.

(Note: If someone did say that you have puny earlobes, don't let their rudeness get to you. Maybe you do. And so what? Maybe that person has a puny heart!)

Go easy on the person in the mirror.

It takes a long time to get comfortable with your looks.

—DYLAN MCDERMOTT

"Beauty to me is being comfortable in your own skin," said Gwyneth Paltrow.

If you're thinking, *Comfortable? Easy for Dylan McDermott and Gwyneth Paltrow to say!* you do have a point.

But you *can* get comfortable with how you look, even if you'll never be mistaken for either of those actors.

And once you're comfortable with yourself, others feel comfortable with you.

If, however, you obsess about your nose or toes, lips or hips, pecs or specs, eyes or size, abs or flabs—you are wasting good brain cells.

Start liking your reflection. Even if it takes practice.

Step one is to smile at the mirror instead of frown. See? Don't you already look (and feel) better?

No one has the perfect face or perfect body. If you have a little scar or a gap between your teeth, or a toe that's funny-shaped, or unruly eyebrows, hey, that's part of what makes you, you. Someone who loves you may even adore that gap or those brows.

Angelina Jolie said, "I find flaws attractive." Me, too. Here's to imperfection!

Give yourself a thumbs-up.

I always felt a bit small in the chest area.
Usually I am okay with that, but sometimes I wish
I had the power to make them smaller or bigger.

—SANDRA BULLOCK

E ven movie stars, male and female, occasionally wish they looked different.

"I'd like to wake up in the morning and look like Brad Pitt, but I don't," confessed Anthony Hopkins.

Yet the ideal is to be okay with *your* looks: your height, your shape, your voice, your face, your hair, yourself.

Have you ever considered spending thousands of dollars so that a knife-wielding doctor could make complicated and potentially dangerous additions or subtractions to your growing body? Think again! Changing your attitude is much more sensible and less risky than changing your body.

"Why not be oneself? That is the whole secret of a successful appearance. If one is a greyhound, why try to look like a Pekinese?" asked British poet Edith Sitwell.

Do what you can to look your best, then start believing Billy Crystal's line: "You look maahhhvelous."

The goal isn't to look a certain way; it's to accept yourself.

Scarlett O'Hara was not beautiful, but men seldom realized it when caught by her charm as the Tarleton twins were.

—margaret mitchell

The first line of *Gone With the Wind* surprised me. Scarlett O'Hara, *not* beautiful! Who knew?

Yet we could all cite sexy babes who aren't cookie-cutter cute, and hot guys who aren't tall, dark, and handsome.

There are many ways to be attractive. And personality beats appearance every time. Being caring and confident counts more than being slim or zit-free.

"Exuberance is beauty," wrote William Blake.

Whether you're male or female, classically attractive or not, if you can manage to feel good, you'll wind up looking good.

How you act is more important than how you look.

If we could give every individual the right amount of
nourishment and exercise, not too little and not too much,
we would have found the safest way to health.

–Hippocrates

H ippocrates, excuse me, *Dr.* Hippocrates, uttered the above in Greek over two *millennia* ago. Yet we pitiful humans still have a tough time eating right and getting exercise.

Cameron Diaz said, "I think women's bodies are beautiful no matter what shape." And hey, some of us like men's bodies, too. ☺

Thanks to luck and genes, your shape is partly a given. But whether you are naturally stocky or a bit of a beanpole, you *can* control what shape you're in. How? Exercise!

Actress Renée Zellweger runs. "It's my alone time. I depend on it," she said. "When I'm frustrated, I think it out by pounding it into the cement."

How do you stay fit? Do you have a sport or routine? Do you run? Swim? Snowboard? Ski? Do crunches? Yoga? Do you walk or bike instead of always taking cars or buses or subways?

If you are both a couch potato and a potato chip fan, you're in danger of becoming potato-like. Don't let this happen. Obesity, while all too common in America, is dangerous to your health.

Stay active. Outside or inside. Alone or with friends or on a team. You owe it to your body. And you'll feel better, stronger, more energetic.

P.S. Don't overdo it, either. The goal is to stay in shape, not spend your life at the gym or become compulsive about working out.

Keep moving.

A toast! To toast! I love toast!

—mel Brooks

lot of people are seriously confused about the whole eating thing. But it's not that complicated.

Your car needs fuel and your body needs food. Your car won't work if you don't put the right fuel in it, and your body won't work if you don't put nutritious food in it. Right now, while you're growing, you need extra energy.

So feed your body: Eat your breakfast. Have lunch. Enjoy dinner. If you skip a meal, you'll be ravenous at the next. Your body works best if you insert reasonable amounts of healthful food into it at regular intervals.

Do not, however, overfeed or undernourish your body. Don't have a candy bar before lunch or fast food before dinner or a sundae before bed.

Think variety, too. Wait, I'm thinking *variety* and wondering who said, "Variety is the spice of life." Hang on, I'll be right back—

Poet William Cowper. (Thank you, *Bartlett's Familiar Quotations!*)

Of course, when he wrote, "Variety's the very spice of life" (complete with that "very"), he was not referring to food.

But I am. You should eat all over the food pyramid (bread, rice, cereal, pasta; meat, chicken, fish, eggs, beans; milk, cheese, yogurt; fruits and vegetables). Because if you eat nothing but Whoppers, canned soup, and macaroni and cheese, you may feel full, but your poor body will be desperate for nutrients. Which could mean fatigue today . . . and brittle bones tomorrow.

Girls especially—drink milk to get your calcium! And vegetarians, male and female—think beans, nuts, tofu, cheese, and get your protein!

Eat well.

41

My doctor told me to stop having intimate dinners for four.
Unless there are three other people.
—orson welles

Your body means well. It figures that since you downed a whole bunch of bacon *and* three stacks of syrup-drenched pancakes, well, you were eating extra because you were not planning to eat again for quite a while. Since your body can't burn through all those calories, it cleverly stores them up for later. It may even take some stored-up energy and turn it into nice soft body padding in case of famine.

"Now that we have refrigerators, there is no longer any need to use the human buttock as a food-storage device," humorist Dave Barry pointed out. "But try getting this message through to your body. Try leaning back over your shoulder and shouting at your buttocks, 'HEY BACK THERE! STOP STORING FAT!'"

Rather than count calories, be sensible. Make sure your brain is checking in on what your mouth is up to.

George Bernard Shaw wrote, "There is no love sincerer than the love of food." Sometimes it can feel that way. But if you catch yourself eating compulsively, go for a walk. Or brush your teeth. Or chew sugarless gum.

You want a cookie? Have a cookie. But don't burrow your way to the bottom of the cookie jar. Better yet, put your will power to use once in a while, rather than test it all day long at home.

Note: If you inhale huge quantities of nutritious food (not junk food) and you're in shape, not to worry. Many active teens have voracious appetites. It's just the double orders of fries and boatloads of buttered popcorn that get people into trouble.

You don't have to join the clean plate club.

We lived for days on nothing but food and water.

Before I address alcohol (which I'll do in precisely fifteen pages), I want to confess that, tolerant easygoing person that I am, I am shockingly anti-soda.

I first started answering letters from teenagers before you were a zygote. Hundreds and hundreds of those letters have been from miserable teens desperate to lose weight.

If you drink sugary soda, the easiest way to lose weight is to stop.

When you're thirsty, your parched body is already dehydrated, so by all means, drink. Drink juice, which is packed with vitamins, or milk which is *essential* for strong bones, or good old-fashioned water. "Water, taken in moderation, cannot hurt anybody," Mark Twain quipped.

But soda can. Having a sugary soda is like having a liquid dessert. Swilling empty calories all day long is like eating candy (and taking caffeine) all day long. If you are overweight, start noticing how much high fructose corn syrup with food coloring you drink. Then try switching to flavored club soda, or better still, delicious, pure, free, readily available H_2O, which is great for keeping your whole system running smoothly.

Hit the water fountain.

43

I have dieted continuously for the last two decades
and lost a total of 758 pounds. By all calculations,
I should be hanging from a charm bracelet.

—ErMa BOMBECK

"Diets are the root of all evil," said Roseanne. "They are the reason everyone is fat."

Everyone is *not* fat, but diets definitely *are* a bad way to go.

I hope you feel fine and look fine and are smarter than the Mira Sorvino character in *Romy and Michele's High School Reunion* who said, "I've been trying this new fat free diet I invented. All I've had to eat for the past six days are gummy bears, jelly beans, and candy corns."

Ridiculous diets are ridiculous. Fad diets don't work, and diet pills can be dangerous. Have you noticed the fine print in diet pill ads? "Side effects may include dizziness, stomach bleeding, hair loss . . ." and "Results not typical." Look again at the before-after photos. It's not thick versus thin. It's frumpy, frowning people versus chic and smiling ones. The comparison is bogus!

Anything that seems too good to be true probably is. And people who lose weight fast often gain it back fast.

Some people weigh themselves every day. I don't even own a scale because I don't want to start each day with a number and then worry if I'm half a pound heavier than I was the night before. (Boring! Brain drain!)

If you truly believe—or know—that you need to trim down for your health and appearance, get serious about exercising and modifying your eating habits now, while you're young. Start with my Simple S Suggestion: Cut back on Soda, Snacks, Seconds, and Sweets.

Don't diet. Eat a little less and exercise a little more.

You can either destroy your spirit or you can love yourself just the way you are.

—Camryn Manheim

"It is astonishing to me how women hate themselves so much because of their weight," said actress Camryn Manheim.

"I don't have to be a size two to be sexy," said Jennifer Lopez.

Right. The important question is *who* you are, not *what* you weigh.

Girls don't have to be a size two. (Marilyn Monroe was a size fourteen!) And guys don't have to have rippling stomachs.

Are your expectations out of whack?

Women, men, teens, and even kids sometimes look at magazines, commercials, and bus ads and forget that *they* aren't supposed to look like that. Models are expected to have those chests, abs, and tummies. It's their job to be buff or voluptuous. That's what they get paid for.

You don't expect yourself to throw like a ballplayer or operate like a surgeon or entertain like a comedian. So why expect yourself to look like an airbrushed model or bodybuilder? Why hold yourself to such standards? Why buy in to inane media pressure? There are lots of ways to look great. And not everyone prefers beefy guys or underweight girls anyway.

Have you ever wished you could be a model? Consider these words from Kate Moss: "I ———ing hate it. How many pictures have I done by the Eiffel Tower?"

You're more than your measurements.

The majority of adolescents I speak to look at size 2 as normal when in fact the average adolescent is a size 12.

—Dr. Ira Sacker

Many people, female and male, have struggled with anorexia (starving oneself), bulimia (binging, then purging), and compulsive eating. Eating disorders are common, dangerous, and, in extreme cases, fatal. They can become habits that run or ruin your life. Anorexics can literally go from slim to skinny to skeletal to dead. Bulimics often don't lose weight at all but throwing up damages their esophagus, gums, teeth, and bodies. And too many teens abuse diet pills, laxatives, and diuretics.

Are eating disorders more common among girls? Yes. Are guys immune? No.

If a friend has stopped eating and is looking bony but considers herself or himself fat, try to help the person recognize the problem and get out of denial. Some people are able to get back on track by themselves. Most need professional help, counseling, and a support group to recover and prevent relapses.

The person with the problem should try to go three days eating "normally" or fairly healthfully. (A slice of apple and a leaf of lettuce is not enough of a lunch; half of a cake is too much dessert.) If the person cannot, she or he should talk to a nurse, doctor, or trusted adult, call a hot line, or log on to the American Anorexia/Bulimia Association's website: www.aabainc.org.

If it's a friend, be sympathetic but stubborn. Your friend needs you.

If it's you, get help now. Don't keep hurting yourself. Your body needs to last your whole life, and the sooner you start eating well again, the better.

Respect yourself.

Sleep is the best cure for waking troubles.
—miguel de cervantes

John Steinbeck said, "It is a common experience that a problem difficult at night is resolved in the morning after the committee of sleep has worked on it."

Ever notice how cranky people get when they're tired? Maybe even you?

Babies and senior citizens wake up with the roosters. Most teens can sleep until noon. You need sleep because you're growing. A few schools have tried to accommodate teenage circadian rhythms (body clocks) by scheduling late-morning classes, but in most schools, class starts frighteningly early, ready or not.

Unless you're okay with yawning through second period and drooling, facedown, during fourth, you have to get enough sleep. Midnight to 6:30 won't cut it. You need a bare minimum of eight hours a night, and nine or ten is even better. So get into bed at a decent hour—even if you're a night owl. And when possible, tuck yourself in extra early and sleep in on weekends to offset your sleep debt.

Having trouble falling asleep? Don't drink caffeine after school or take weekday naps. Exercise, but not at night. Avoid action-packed TV or family feuds before bed. Instead, relax in a hot bath, or read a novel or children's book, or play not-too-loud music. Drink hot milk. And remind yourself that resting counts—you are not under pressure to fall asleep instantly.

Sleep tight.

Dreaming permits each and every one of us to be quietly and safely insane every night of our lives.

—Dr. William Dement

One more great thing about sleep: When you're asleep, you get to dream. And dreaming is fun—and good for you and even informative. Dreams can help you understand what (or whom!) you're thinking about.

"Sleep is when all the unsorted stuff comes flying out as from a dustbin upset in a high wind," said William Golding.

If you think you never dream, you're mistaken. Everyone dreams. If you have trouble recalling your dreams, give yourself a few minutes upon waking to try to piece them back together. Keep a pencil and pad by your bed and write down, without censoring, whatever you remember. (Dreams scatter when you have to jump right up or when they feel judged.)

I don't believe that dreams predict the future or hold the key to all your troubles. But it can be interesting to pay attention to your dreams—the flying dreams, the falling dreams. And talking about a dream can sometimes help you talk about—and unravel—a problem.

P.S. If you dreamed you kissed your best friend's main squeeze or your hot young teacher, don't sweat it. Dreams aren't supposed to be 100 percent appropriate, and the characters in your dreams may be symbolic stand-ins for entirely different people.

Sweet dreams.

W hen you hit puberty, puberty hits back.

You don't have to be squeaky clean every single day, but you don't want to stink. And body odor sometimes happens after human beings reach double digits.

Over the years, I've gotten deluged with letters about B.O. Not the letter writer's B.O.—always someone else's. "This guy in my class wears the same shirt every day and *smells!*" "How can we tell our friend that if she doesn't start using deodorant, *we're* going to start using gas masks?"

Don't get paranoid—but do stay clean. Shower in the morning or when you've been sweating, and wash your underarms with soap. Use deodorant. And wear clean shirts. Showering once a day or every other day is okay. Showering less often is—well, you don't want anyone writing a letter about *you,* do you?

As for aromatic friends, if you can't be direct, be gentle. Lend this book with this page dog-eared. Or sneak a deodorant into the person's gym locker. Or comment on a product you bought. Or mention a person at camp who finally came around. Or say, "It's because we're friends that I'm telling you . . ." Or ask what deodorant the person uses. Or recommend yours. Or just say, "Here, try this!"

Rubber duckies are optional; bathing is not.

Pay attention to your hair because everyone else will.

—Hillary Rodham Clinton

I f you want tips on hair care or styles, sorry, you'll have to check out other books and magazines. I don't even own a blow-dryer.

I can suggest shampooing often, brushing your hair every morning (but not every minute), and getting your hair cut only by people who know what they are doing. Do what you can to help your hair look good. Then, since you have only twenty-four hours a day, get on with it. Don't let hair care eat up too much of your precious time.

Should you color your hair? Maybe in a few decades when you go gray! If you really want to experiment with color, at least don't be naive about it. Your own lighter or darker hair will soon come peeking out beneath the yellow or pink locks, and you'll either have to keep coloring or resign yourself to looking temporarily two-toned. (Lots of teens have gone to lots of trouble undoing a look they couldn't wait to do. And many dark-haired teens have been disappointed to find that the highlights that looked lemony in July turned orangey in October.) Still dying to dye? Check out less permanent products that wash out fast.

Last tip. Beware of hair-smushing hats if you'll be going from outside to inside!

Even good people have bad hair days.

When you're smiling, the whole world smiles with you.
—JOE GOODWIN AND LARRY SHAY

Many children have adorable straight baby teeth . . . then crowded crooked adult ones. Are your teeth getting straightened? Back in the olden days, braces were silvery, retainers were pinkish, and there was nothing remotely cool about any of it.

Braces still aren't a reason to celebrate, but at least they come in different colors (including clear), and the wiring can sometimes be behind your teeth. As for retainers, you can pick one with a design on it (or not) and you can ask your orthodontist about wearing it only at night.

Braces are common, and they come off eventually, so be patient. Meantime, keep wax and aspirin on hand for those long hours after your orthodontist tweaks and tightens the hardware.

Whether you have braces or not, brush your teeth: twice a day minimum, or you'll get tooth decay. Find a dentist you like (I recommend my high school friend David Binder in Manhattan) and go twice a year for cleanings and checkups. At home, floss after brushing. You'll be amazed (and horrified) by what the brush misses. Finally, don't spend your days chewing sugary gum, sucking lollipops, eating candy, or downing sugar water—see my soda diatribe eight pages back.

While we're talking mouths, let me add that if you brush your teeth regularly with toothpaste, you should not have to worry about bad breath. But to be on the safe side, stay away from onions, garlic, and spicy foods, especially if you think your mouth and someone else's might be getting together.

Take care of your teeth; you'll be needing them.

I never forget a face. However, in your case,
I'll be glad to make an exception.
—GrOUCHO marx

I f you have bad skin, you're hardly alone.

It helps to wash your face religiously, eat healthfully, drink loads of water, get lots of exercise and sleep, and keep your hands and hair away from your forehead, nose, and chin.

Even if you're doing everything right, you may still have a case of pizza face. Should you pick those pimples? No! Don't invite today's blemish to become tomorrow's scar. Instead, press a hot, wet washcloth to your face, repeating as needed, and experiment with acne products from swabs to ointments to cover-ups.

Remember, too, that the whole school is not noticing your nose. They have their own worries to think about (and their own noses to worry about).

If necessary, consult a dermatologist. I did. He or she can prescribe medication for your skin and answer questions about warts, moles, rashes, scars, tattoo removal, etc. If you ever have a mole that morphs and suddenly changes color or shape, get it checked right away.

Oh, and don't kid around with the sun. It might feel good to bake like a cookie in an oven, but if you don't protect yourself, the sun will broil your skin in no time. Wear a hat and use sunscreen with an SPF of at least 15 to protect your skin from sunburn now and skin cancer later.

You don't care about their zits;
they don't care about yours.

My one advice with tattoos is never write names on your body.

Never, never, never, never!

CARRÉ OTIS

The above is brought to you by a model who graced the covers of *Vogue* and *Harper's Bazaar* as well as the inside of *Sports Illustrated* swimsuit issues.

If you can't for the life of you imagine why anyone would say such a thing, skip right ahead to the Relationships chapter.

In *Tattoo Artist*, Norman Rockwell painted a sailor getting his arm tattooed. The names Sadie, Rosietta, Ming Fu, Mimi, Olga, and Sing Lee have all been crossed out, and a seventh name, Betty, is being carefully added on.

Are you thinking, *I'd never tattoo a name on my shoulder—but I am considering a fire-breathing dragon . . .* ? Remind yourself that your dragon would still be exhaling flames when you're twenty and forty and sixty and eighty.

Sometimes today's fad is tomorrow's regret.

Love doesn't always last forever; tattoos do.

Clothes make the man. Naked people have little or
no influence on society.

Anything goes: T-shirts, jeans . . . you'll fit right in.

But if you want to stand out, clothes can help. "Fashion allows us to be anything we want to be, without saying a word," said model Tyra Banks.

First impressions count and people do make fair and unfair assumptions about others according to what they're wearing. If you see a woman with a short-short skirt or sky-high heels, or a man with eyebrow rings and nose studs, you probably assume the person is not, say, a pediatrician, banker, or fifth-grade teacher.

Have you ever rented *Grease* or *Tootsie*? They're all about image.

Because your clothes are talking for you, make sure you agree with what they're saying. Your closet probably includes blue jeans and black pants. But what else is in it?

Your clothes can be hand-me-downs or cutting edge. They don't have to be new. They just have to be You.

What are your clothes saying?

My mother is very focused on beauty. . . . Her advice was
always about making my features more than they were:
'Always outline your lips, dear. They're so tiny.'
You got to the point where you felt like you were
the ugliest duckling on the planet.
—Jennifer aniston

Sorry, guys, feel free to skip this one brief page. It's about makeup. Girls, have you been collecting lip glosses and eye shadows? This can be a pleasure and a rite of passage. But try not to go overboard or get hooked on expensive name brands.

There's a lot to be said for the low-maintenance look, for feeling attractive no matter what you are (or aren't!) wearing.

If you've ever wondered why women's magazines go on and on about makeup, it's not because there is anything astonishingly new in the world of pastel powders. It's because cosmetics companies *buy* the colorful ads that provide the money that keeps magazines in the black. So magazines have to keep cosmetics companies happy by making it seem as if makeup makes the woman. It doesn't. Never has. In fact, too much makeup can hide a woman's beautiful face.

Sandra Bullock said, "We wear these clothes and this makeup for other women more than for men. Men don't care. They just want us naked."

I threw that quote in for any guys who stuck it out and read this page. And now I'll apologize for the stereotyping. I know that, fortunately, we've come a long way, and most young men look at most young women as whole people, not just potential conquests.

Makeup: Less is more.

One of the fundamentals that is almost
sacred to me is posture.
—tiger WOODS

Posture matters—on and off the putting green.

If you're slouching or hunched, you won't look as good or as confident as you will if you stand up with shoulders back and stomach in.

Good posture now also means fewer backaches later.

You can learn this in sports, gymnastics, dance, or yoga class, or you can just start becoming more aware of how you carry your body.

Stand tall.

I am militant about drugs. You want to do 'em?
You're out of my life.
—Sarah Michelle Gellar

Drugs are dangerous, addictive, and against the law. If you get busted, you could wind up with a record. Or in prison. Or hooked. Or dead. Even if you smoke "just" marijuana and don't get caught, you can puff years away getting high while friends are getting jobs or degrees, marrying, or moving on with their lives.

Drugs can rearrange your priorities, distort your values, and sidetrack you. Some teens abuse sleeping pills or swallow Ritalin by the handful and think that those don't count as drugs. They do. Drugs are to be taken according to doctors' directions, not ones you make up as you go along.

Courtney Love said, "Drugs are dumb and self-indulgent." She should know. Her husband, musician Kurt Cobain of Nirvana, committed suicide while on heroin.

Some teens think, *Hey, I'm just curious. A little harmless experimenting. Nothing big.* But how can they know what's in the pill in their hand? How can they know they won't get caught—or caught up in the swirl of drugs? How can they even know they won't have a bad drug experience?

If your friends use drugs, don't join in. If you have a friend who is off-balance because of drugs, don't abandon that person. Consider, alone or with someone else, saying, "I'm worried about you." There *is* such a thing as positive peer pressure.

Musician Neil Young sang, "I've seen the needle and the damage done." Beatle George Harrison said of Haight-Ashbury in 1967, "It was full of horrible spotty drop-out kids on drugs and . . . I thought I couldn't put that into my brain anymore."

Use your brain. Don't mess with it.

I was so insecure when I first started out, that I would drink
way too much alcohol. If I have any regrets, it's when I look
in the mirror in the morning with no makeup on,
and I curse those days of boozing and binging.

—cameron Diaz

"I think this calls for a drink' has long been one of our national slogans," wrote James Thurber.

It's one thing for an adult to have a glass of wine with dinner. It's another for a teen to do four shots of tequila at a club. Too many people who are underage overdrink. Alcohol puts you at risk—and not just for blotchy skin. Some kids drink and vomit. Others drink, drive, and have car wrecks. Others get busted by the police or have unprotected sex. A few get alcohol poisoning and die. And some start a lifelong drinking habit that becomes a serious problem and a burden on themselves and others. (Ben Affleck was in rehab by the time he realized it was "kind of depressing to be bombed at three in the morning.")

If you are at a party and you don't want to drink alcohol, sip at a plastic cup of water or juice or seltzer. No one will even notice or care. Closer friends may even appreciate it if you'll be their designated driver.

You can also try to find friends whose idea of a good time does not involve drinking and passing out on the sofa.

Drinking to get drunk is beyond stupid. It's dangerous. Being out-and-out drunk isn't even fun. When the room is spinning and you think you might throw up and you're slurring your words and you're not sure how you'll get home (much less what you'll tell your parents when you get there), you really will wish you'd passed on the punch.

Pass on the punch.

I can see why my parents started smoking. It looked glamorous up there on the big screen—some studly movie star lighting two cigarettes and handing one to the vixen at his side.

But that was *before* people knew that smoking is indisputably linked to lung disease, emphysema, and cancer, and that it wrecks people's health.

If you start smoking, it's hard to quit. Nicotine is addictive, and cigarettes are little wrapped-up packets of nicotine—a clever streamlined nicotine delivery system.

If you start smoking to be cool, you should know that while a few people may find you more approachable because of your inhaling and exhaling, many others are likely to keep their distance.

If someone offers you a cigarette, say no. Or even "No thanks" or "I'm allergic" or "I don't like the taste." But don't pick up a smelly, expensive habit that yellows your teeth, stinks up your clothes, makes it harder for you to run or excel at sports, and could eventually kill you. Most American adult smokers would like to quit smoking cigarettes. (My parents both managed to.) Do you really want to start?

Every day thousands of the tobacco companies' best customers are dying off. Replacing those customers should be their problem, not yours.

You don't have to look down on people who smoke. But please don't start lighting up yourself. Don't pollute your body. Don't inhale harmful addictive chemicals. It's so not worth it.

Too smart to smoke.

When I was younger, I did self-mutilate.
I'd be upset, so I'd do it, and it would calm me down.
It's a horrible way to feel better . . . I got over that.
—CHRISTINA RICCI

There are many ways to hurt yourself.

If you are doing something self-destructive, please get help.

If you can't end a bad habit on your own, tell a trusted adult. Call a doctor. Call a hot line anonymously (toll-free numbers are free and don't show up on phone bills). At least, seek information online.

The first step to getting better is admitting you have a problem. If you can reach out to a friend or relative or professional, you're already heading in the right direction.

Counselors and therapists have heard it all. They won't laugh or judge or spread your news. They will help you stop starving yourself, drugging yourself, making yourself sick, pulling out your hair, or cutting yourself.

They'll help you heal.

If you look, you'll find that there is always someone willing and able to help you—every step of the way. Once you've taken that first step, keep going! Don't look back. It's hard to stop a harmful habit, but many people have done so, and you can, too.

Don't hurt yourself.

I seldom think about my limitations, and they never make me
sad. Perhaps there is just a touch of yearning at times,
but it is vague, like a breeze among flowers.

—Helen Keller

H elen Keller gets an A plus for attitude. Once she unlocked her voracious desire to learn and achieve, she never let being deaf and blind
hold her back. Neither did musician Stevie Wonder, who said, "Just
because a man lacks the use of his eyes doesn't mean he lacks vision."

A lot of people have disabilities or conditions that others don't understand, but the more you accept yourself, the more others will accept you.
If you are blind or hearing-impaired or paralyzed and are self-conscious
about it, others will pick up on that nervousness and have a hard time
feeling at ease with you. If you can relax, others will relax.

No matter what the circumstances, it takes a while to feel good in
your own skin, and it's a goal worth striving toward—especially if you
think something sets you apart. Something sets all of us apart.

Learn all you can about how to take care of yourself, and visit chat
rooms where you can meet teens who have met any special challenges
you may face. (Share your stories—but not your phone number or
address.)

If you have, or might have, a learning disability, talk to your parents
or school specialists about getting extra help and support. Maybe medication or behavior changes can help. Or maybe you just follow the beat
of a different drummer.

What's important is to keep counting your blessings. We all have
challenges and reasons to be thankful.

Everyone has strengths and weaknesses.

Be careful of reading health books.
You might die of a misprint.
—mark twain

Health food? "I just hate health food," said chef and foodie Julia Child, who also said, "Life itself is the proper binge."

Rather than obsess about your health, take care of yourself.

You're getting older. Go ahead and try the beets and taste the salmon and sample the pine nuts. Take brisk walks. Breathe fresh air. Get enough sleep.

We are mammals, and if our bodies are not in good working order, it's much harder to think about friends, relationships, school, family, work, and all the stuff that makes up the rest of this book—and the rest of your life.

So don't obsess about your body. Take care of it.

Pore over health books? Nah. Just live healthily.

FRIENDS

If I could do it over, I'd have friends.

—bY COBB

I was about to start this chapter when friends invited me to meet them at a Chinese restaurant. Perfect timing! I was hungry and I needed a break because I wasn't sure quite where to begin.

Should I write about the value of friendship? About making and keeping friends? About talking and listening? About honesty? Popularity? Gossip? About how you can't be everybody's friend?

Should I quote Indian leader Indira Gandhi, who said, "You can't shake hands with a clenched fist"? Or the Beatles, who sang, "Life is very short, and there's no time for fussing and fighting, my friend"? Or Dave Matthews Band: "I'll lean on you and you lean on me and we'll be okay"?

It felt good to leave it all behind and concentrate on my own friends (as well as dumplings, fried rice, and sautéed spinach).

Then the bill came, along with the fortune cookies. I cracked open my cookie and read: "The secret to good friends is no secret to you."

Roughly translated, I figured that meant: "C'mon, Carol, quit your stalling. You know about friendship, so get to work."

And here I am, back at my desk ready to tell you—or perhaps just remind you—about the ins and outs of friendship.

Where to start? With this quote from Samuel Johnson: "Be a friend. The rest will follow."

If you're not making friends, you're making a mistake.

A friend is a present you give yourself.

—ROBERT LOUIS STEVENSON

F riends? "They just make life more fun," said Drew Barrymore. You don't need to have a best friend. You don't need to be popular. But you do need a few friends to make fun times more fun and bad times less bad.

"Friendship is unnecessary, like philosophy, like art," wrote C. S. Lewis, author of *The Chronicles of Narnia*. "It has no survival value; rather it is one of those things that give value to survival."

While you can't always choose your family or neighbors or teachers or classmates, you *can* choose your friends. You can find the people you like who will like you back. You can join after-school activities with people who care about what you care about. You can try to be friendly (open, upbeat, fun, engaging), which draws people to you, rather than unfriendly (distanced, negative, snobby, indifferent), which puts others off. You can become more interested in others, which makes others more interested in you.

Friends help you feel connected to the world, good about yourself, and more lighthearted.

"Adolescence is often a painfully lonely time," said author Lois Lowry. For some teens, that's true. But it doesn't have to be for you. And as Shakespeare wrote:

But if the while I think on thee, my friend,
All losses are restor'd and sorrows end.

Give yourself friends.

> *Normally I'm shy. It takes me ages to open up*
> *and trust somebody.*
> —BRITNEY SPEARS

Shy? Britney??

"I'm always nervous to meet people I admire," said Tom Cruise. Nervous? Tom??

If Britney and Tom have bouts of bashfulness, no wonder the rest of us get tongue-tied.

It's natural to feel awkward with someone new, so practice being friendly with people you're comfortable with. Receptionists, neighbors, relatives, bus drivers, cafeteria workers. Say hi and meet the person's eyes. Give a compliment or ask a question. Most people are way more anxious about what *they* are going to say than what *you* are going to say. Yet if you don't say anything at all, you can come off not as shy but as stuck-up.

"The way to overcome shyness is to become so wrapped up in something that you forget to be afraid," said former first lady Lady Bird Johnson, who had to talk to all sorts of intimidating politicians, kings, and queens. She may have expounded upon her passion: the glory of wildflowers.

What are *your* passions? If you know a lot about a particular band or actor or athlete, you can talk confidently about that subject. If there is a club at school where everyone is buzzing about a jazz concert or theater revue or service project, you can join that club—and that conversation.

Take a chance. The only person holding you back is you.

Shy? That was then; this is now.

There is only one rule for being a good talker: Learn to listen.
—CHRISTOPHER MORLEY

T ell me about it.

No, really. Those four little words can launch a friendship.

Try them on someone today.

After all, if someone says, "I saw that movie," or "I had a great weekend," and you say, "Really?" or "Cool," the conversation can end. But if you say, "Tell me about it," it keeps going.

For shy people, becoming a good listener is a great way to make friends.

For talkative types, becoming a good listener is equally essential. George Bernard Shaw described a blabbermouth this way: "She had lost the art of conversation, but not, unfortunately, the power of speech." Greek philosopher Democritus said, "To do all the talking and not be willing to listen is a form of greed."

I know *you* are not greedy. So don't just hear people. Listen to what they say. And also what they *don't* say.

"A friend," said Toni Morrison, "gathers all the pieces and gives them back in the right order."

Shhh . . . listen.

When people show you who they are, believe them.

—maya angelou

Don't try to be friends with Annie because she's so popular or Andrew because he's always free. Think about whom you want to be friends with and why.

Yogi Berra said, "You can observe a lot by watching." Start noticing what people reveal about themselves. Some teens gulp a Gatorade in the park and throw the empty bottle into the bushes. Others pick up discarded litter and place it in the trash. Some people criticize their so-called friends in public. Others defend their friends. Some people lie or steal. Others never would.

Notice how *you* feel with certain classmates. Accepted? Shut out? Excited? Bored? Depressed?

What if a person makes it clear that your company is not welcome? Be glad you found out sooner rather than later. And tell yourself (over and over if necessary) that anyone who doesn't appreciate you is not worth your time.

Do you have a "friend" who depresses you? How much do you want to invest in the friendship? "Misery is a communicable disease," said dancer Martha Graham. In *The Amazing Adventures of Cavalier and Klay,* a Michael Chabon character laments, "I spend ten minutes listening to him, I go away with a full tank of gloom, it lasts me all day."

If one of your friends brings you down, at least make sure you have friends who lift you up. Think about what effect *you* have on people, too.

Some friendships are made randomly—by chance.

Others are made deliberately—by choice.

Choose; don't just get chosen.

No act of kindness, no matter how small, is ever wasted.

−aesop

I personally think we developed language because of our deep inner need to complain," quipped playwright Jane Wagner.

Everybody gets bummed out, and sometimes one encouraging word is all it takes—or would take—to help a person feel better.

Imagine: It's Saturday night, you're alone, and you don't feeeeeeeel like sitting in front of the TV. So you go online and your mailbox is . . . empty. Then someone sends you an e-mail or instant message.

A little "hi" can make a big difference and make you go from ☹ to ☺.

While it's lucky when someone asks, "Are you okay?" or delivers a verbal hug (or real hug or cyber hug) precisely when you need it, sometimes you have to ask for support. You have to say, "I had a bad day," or "Do you have a minute?" No, you don't want to always come off as needy or complaining, but, yes, you're entitled to ask for encouragement once in a while.

Mark Twain said, "The best way to cheer yourself up is to cheer someone else up." It's true. So be generous with mini pep talks. They are fun, easy, and friendship-building. Instead of just forwarding jokes online, type out personal notes with compliments or support. You'll feel better and will probably get some "valentines" back.

One match lights up a room.

Do unto others as you would have them do unto you.

—ᴛʜᴇ BIBLE

George Bernard Shaw tweaked the golden rule and wrote: "Do not do unto others as you would they should do unto you. Their tastes may not be the same."

Friendship is not one-rule-fits-all. But thoughtfulness always counts. And thinking not just about yourself but about your friend is an excellent way to go. So don't just talk about your weekend—ask about his. And don't just pour yourself some juice—fill her glass, too, or ask if she'd like something else instead.

Be the kind of friend you would want to have.

> *My idea of an agreeable person is*
> *a person who agrees with me.*
> —Benjamin Disraeli

I disagree!

Sure, agreeable people are fun to be around. But would you *really* want friends who nod and laugh no matter what you say? Isn't it better to have friends who can introduce you to new ideas, people, books, magazines, musicians, movies, and points of view? Isn't it better—and more interesting—to have friends who speak their minds?

"Hateful to me as the gates of Hades," Homer wrote, "is he who hides one thing in his mind and speaks another."

What if a friend says, "Which movie should we rent?" then suggests *Shakespeare in Love, Legally Blonde, Animal House,* or *The Princess Bride*? Instead of saying, "Whatever," then resenting your friend for being unable to mind-read, pick one. Same if a friend asks if you want to go for burgers or a slice. It's not rude to say, "Pizza," unless you insist on pizza every time.

Actress Reese Witherspoon said, "I'm not going to shut up. I've earned the right to have an opinion."

So have you. Be good-natured about it, but state your opinion, even (or especially) if it's not the same as everyone else's.

Be agreeable without always agreeing.

This is who I am. Not everybody has to like it.

—LISA KUDROW

Y ou don't like everybody. Not everybody will like you. And that's okay. Some people may be jealous of you or put off by the way you act or talk or dress.

"A tough lesson in life," said TV newsman Dan Rather, "is that not everybody wishes you well."

When people are not friendly, let that be their problem, not yours. Focus on the people who are your friends. And on pleasing yourself.

Who'd want to be everyone's cup of tea?

Do not brag. If you brag, you may as well be wearing a sandwich board that says, "I am massively insecure."
—CYNTHIA HEIMEL

While it's good to have healthy self-esteem, it's bad to brag. Remember when Peter Pan tells the three Darling children to "Think lovely thoughts," so that they, too, can soar off to Never-Neverland? He swoops around their London nursery singing,

I fly and I'm all over the place,
You fly and you fall flat on your face.

Well, I love Peter Pan, but he can get away with things that regular people can't.

Like flying. And boasting.

So don't try this at home. If you try to fly, you'll flop. And if you brag (about grades, clothes, famous friends, or R-rated exploits), most people won't believe you, and others will be put off.

Not worth it.

Besides, "The less people speak of their greatness, the more we think of it," as Lord Francis Bacon pointed out.

If you just *have* to brag, brag to your parents or grandparents—they may actually want you to make a short story long.

Let friends hear you bragging about *them*: "Did you see that goal? She was incredible!" or "Have you heard him play bass? He's amazing!"

Your friends will quietly eat it up, and you'll feel good, too. (Next time, they might even compliment you!)

Confident, yes. Boastful, no.

When shall we three meet again?

In thunder, lightning, or in rain?

—WILLIAM SHAKESPEARE

Three? Three can be trickier than two.

Sometimes threesomes work. But often three's a crowd. Over the years, I've gotten hundreds of letters from readers saying they feel left out or stuck in the middle or upset about having to compete for a friend's attention.

Do you have triangle troubles? When three friends hang out, do tensions rise, jealousies flare, or feelings get bruised? This can happen with three girls or three guys, and also when the equation is "couple plus one." You like hanging with your best friend and your sweetie? Great. But each of them would probably like some alone time with you—and without the sidekick.

Try to see, or at least talk to, your friends one at a time. Or add a fourth to the mix. Don't just keep hoping that everyone will start magically getting along.

And don't let anyone make you choose between your friends—there's enough of you to go around.

Fact is, your friends don't even *have* to like one another. And you are all allowed to have other relationships. It's even smart, because what if a friend moves or if two friends grow apart?

An advantage of seeing one friend at a time is that conversations can run deeper, and intense conversations are a crucial part of real friendship—unless they're always about the missing third person! So try a tête-à-tête, instead of tête-à-tête-à-têtes.

Two's company. Three's complicated.

Punctuality is the virtue of the bored.

—Evelyn Waugh

"**N**ever be on time; you waste too much time waiting for the other fellow," Mark Twain joked. Yet punctuality shows that you respect other people's time—not just your own. When friends know you are punctual, they become more punctual and try not to make you wait.

If you realize that you're going to be late, make it by five minutes, not twenty. And phone ahead.

Arriving early is not ideal either. If you get to your boyfriend's parents' party early, you'll find frantic half-dressed people and you may get stuck setting the table (not that you shouldn't offer to help anyway). If you arrive at your girlfriend's early, you may get the third degree ("What movie are you seeing?" "When will you be back?" "Where do you live?") from her parents while she's putting on lip gloss (not that you shouldn't chat them up anyway).

Meeting friends outside? Take a book, and if possible, a cell phone—in case plans change. Avoid meeting on a corner since waiting on the street isn't as comfortable as waiting in a coffee shop or bookstore (pick a specific section!).

Do you have a friend who is always late? Arrange to meet at your home so you won't be drumming your fingers. If the movie starts at 7:30, plan to meet at the theater at 7:10—not 7:25. Or plan to meet inside, and say you'll be sitting on the aisle, in the middle section, stage left.

"Better never than late," said George Bernard Shaw. But he was kidding.

Friends don't make friends waste their time.

Friendships are really life's best souvenirs;
you keep a few from high school, a few from college,
a handful from summer camp.

—LISA BELKIN

I f you've always gone to the same school, your friends may all be classmates. But if you've moved around or been to sleepaway camp, and have taken care of your friendships (by phoning, writing, e-mailing, or visiting), you probably have different friends from different chapters of your life.

It's fun to have new experiences with old friends, but it's also fun to share inside jokes or say, "Remember when we ran through sprinklers and got to school soaked?" or "Remember when I built the Colosseum out of marshmallows and it collapsed two seconds before I gave my report?" or "Remember when we went on that double date and locked ourselves out of the car?"

Awful or embarrassing moments have a way of turning into funny stories, especially when a friend can reminisce with you.

James Parry wrote:

Make new friends, but keep the old;
Those are silver, these are gold.

By the way, I found most quotes in books, newspapers, magazines, plays, websites, and the occasional yearbook, but guess where I found that one? On a box of Celestial Seasonings Mint Magic Tea!

Take care of your friendships. Some may last a lifetime.

Many people will walk in and out of your life,
but only true friends will leave footprints on your heart.
—eleanor roosevelt

"True friendship," said George Washington, "is a plant of slow growth." Friends offer company or comfort. When a friendship is solid, it can outlast romance and thrive without daily, weekly, or even monthly contact.

There are girls and guys you care about or flirt with or say hi to. But true friends are the ones you think about—and who think about you—even when apart. They listen when you're upset and cheer for you when things are going well. With them you can talk about anything. You can also go a year without meeting, then pick up where you left off.

Your true friends? They know you well—and like you anyway! They also want to know *how* (not just *what*) you are doing.

French novelist Honoré de Balzac wrote, "There is one thing about trouble; it teaches us to know our true friends." You can't be everyone's true friend or close friend. But when times are rough, whom *would* you be there for? Who would be there for you?

"Let us be grateful to people who make us happy," wrote French author Marcel Proust, "for they are the charming gardeners who make our souls blossom."

True friends are the keepers.

To keep all your old friends is like keeping all your old clothes.
—Helen Gurley Brown

A Turkish proverb says, "None is so rich as to throw away a friend." But it's impossible to keep adding people to your life without occasionally letting others go. There's not enough time for everybody.

Yet why let someone go for a dumb reason? Just because you're maturing faster or slower than each other doesn't mean you two won't get back in sync. Just because you have been noticed by a popular kid or member of the opposite sex doesn't mean you should abandon your old group. Nor should you ditch an old friend who is going through a hard time—that person may need you.

Are you stuck forever with someone you no longer enjoy? No. You don't have to fake friendship with your summer camp buddy or dad's friend's son if you no longer feel it. But why announce, "I don't want to be friends anymore" when you can just make yourself less available? Why be mean when you can simply be more aloof? Rather than "dump" someone (what an awful verb), just stop making plans, and take your time returning calls or e-mails. The person will probably get the message, without your having to hammer it home—or cause unnecessary hurt.

After all, why pride yourself on your straightforward honesty if what you're really doing is stomping on someone else's ego? Sometimes subtlety is the way to go. (C'mon, wouldn't *you* rather hear, "I'm busy," five times than "I don't like you anymore" even once?)

Besides, you may once again change your mind about this friend, and someday you may want to reconcile.

Don't ditch friends when you can just drift away.

Oh, God, did I want in.
—Claudia Shear

First the good news: While popularity can seem pretty important in middle school, it is somewhat less of a big deal in high school, and it's even less important in college. When you're an adult, it's practically a non-issue. In your school's faculty room, for example, the teachers are *not* vying over who gets to sit next to whom or whispering about who said hi to whom.

Now the bad news: Many students are not open-minded and free-thinking, so when you're a teen, popularity matters.

Me, I wanted "in." In seventh grade, I got briefly confused and started fixating more on Popular Kids than Real Friends. Fortunately, my next-door neighbor and best friend knocked some sense into my head by pointing out (quite rightly) that the cool clique wasn't spending *any* time thinking about me, so why was I spending *so much* time thinking about them? Why was I hovering in their aura hoping for a crumb, a "hi"? Slowly, slowly I got over my yearnings and started focusing *not* on the popular kids (with whom I felt like a wanna-be) but on my actual friends (with whom I felt welcome).

The overwhelming majority of kids in your school are not in that itty bitty popular group. If you are, fine. If you aren't, fine. But if you're all hung up about whether you are or aren't, ask yourself: Which of my friends like me and care about me? Then repeat after me: Real friends are the ones who count, real friends are the ones who count, real friends are the ones who count. . . .

Appreciate those who appreciate you.

There's that insecurity that you're not going to have
the same popularity you did a few years ago.

—A.J McLean

P opularity has a flip side.

★ **You can worry about losing it** (even if you're a celebrity).

★ **Your private life is on display.** If you're visible, you get talked about.

★ **You can feel pressured to conform.** If your group wants to smoke and you don't, or if you like a person (your pal from first grade) but they don't, it takes guts to buck the crowd.

★ **You may feel used.** Is someone talking to you because of who you are—or to gain status, popularity points, or a party invitation?

★ **You can feel alone** because the popular group is a group, yet when you're down, you need one confidante—not a bunch of buddies. ("If I'm such a legend, then why am I so lonely?" asked actress Judy Garland.)

Enough. No need to go overboard pitying the popular. Some popular kids act high and mighty, and need a lesson in humility. Many others are fun and outgoing, and will always have friends.

While there are obvious plusses to being popular, there are also advantages to *not* being popular. For instance: It can be easier to be your own person and pick your own friends (different kids from different groups). And it can be easier to dress however you want, do whatever you want, hang out wherever you want, and be your whole unique colorful surprising self.

Even popularity comes at a price.

We would rather be popular than unpopular,
but it is better to be unpopular than wrong.
—ᵗony Bɭaiᴦ

Although the prime minister of Great Britain was not weighing in on the social life of adolescents, his point is well-taken. At some schools, the popular clique includes a few snobs with fancy cars and a tendency to make jokes at other people's expense. Who needs it?

Of course, no one wants to be *unpopular*. A character in a Gail Carson Levine novel said, "I solved the problem of where to sit at lunch by bringing sandwiches from home. I ate them in the girls' bathroom on the fourth floor as far away from the cafeteria as possible. It was a disgusting place to eat, but in the bathroom I didn't feel so alone because I wasn't in the middle of everybody else having people to talk to."

Withdrawing is a bad idea. But what if you can identify?

★ **Let this book prod you to join a sport or activity,** approach a classmate, meet the new kid in town, whatever. You are only ONE friend away from feeling happier. And that person may be looking for a friend, too.

★ **Ignore taunting.** Why let bullies know they're getting to you?

★ **Consider switching schools.** Drastic, I know. But arriving with a clean slate at a new school may be easier than opening airtight minds.

★ **Hang in there.** Middle school ends. High school ends. And in life (a few brief years away), there's no such thing as popularity, remember? For better and worse, these school days really don't last forever.

Popular? Unpopular? Labels don't last.

After all, in private, we're all misfits.

—LILY TOMLIN

xcuse me, but I just have to make sure that *you* are not out there being a big jerk to people. Tell me that *you*, my esteemed reader, are not teasing some poor soul unmercifully, or using the word "gay" as if it's an insult, or making racist jokes or jeering at someone who is overweight. You're not, right?

Good. I didn't think so.

Atticus told Scout in *To Kill a Mockingbird,* "You never really understand a person until you consider things from his point of view—until you climb into his skin and walk around in it."

No one sets out to be a dork or to be obese or to be a social outcast. So if some people are a little dorky or plump or overly quiet, big deal. They may wish they were cooler, slimmer, or more easygoing, or perhaps that they had some particular advantage that you've had.

Give people a chance. Besides, you never know which of your classmates will improve with age, and which are hitting their peak and heading downhill. You don't know which "nerd" might be the next Nobel laureate—or actor or billionaire. What you *should* know is that it all gets shuffled. Top dogs and underdogs sometimes change places. The élite clique doesn't stay on top forever any more than the school's untouchables stay on the bottom.

Me, I try to be nice to everybody. Not best-friend nice. Just friendly nice.

Writing others off is beneath you.

The most exhausting thing in life is being insincere.
—anne morrow LinDBergH

"A friend is a person with whom I may be sincere. Before him I may think aloud," wrote Ralph Waldo Emerson.

There are a lot of people (such as your parents' pals) with whom you have to lay it on thick with the "Pleased to meet you!" and "How do you do?" Since some adults don't know what to make of teenagers, most are in awe of polite ones. If you butter them up, they may offer baby-sitting jobs, lawns to mow, internships, or connections, as well as tell your parents how charming and mature you are—which can never hurt if you want to buy a DVD and are short three bucks. . . .

But I digress.

The point is, with *real* friends of any age, you can open up and be yourself. You do not have to act phony, fake, or formal. You can admit when you're mad or jealous or insecure or worried or tired. You can confess that you've started flirting online with one person even though you're seeing someone else. You can talk about what you don't like about the person you say you love. You can even talk about what you don't like about yourself.

In short, you can be honest. So can the other person. And uncensored conversation is the mark of a true friendship.

Keep it real.

If we all told what we know of one another, there
would not be four friends in the world.
BLAISE PASCAL

'm not a saint and I don't expect you to be.

If you want to talk about your classmates, that's legal, normal, and sometimes fun. But have a heart. Be discreet about it.

Two thousand years before e-mail, Horace wrote, "A word, once sent abroad, flies irrevocably." Now if you type, "I can't stand Taylor. What a jerk. I seriously don't get why Jess is so obsessed . . ." then press Send, your little message could get forwarded to Taylor or Jess or the whole class. Within seconds.

If you're going to vent about someone, avoid doing it online and never do it on a conference call or within earshot of the person you're dissing. Do it in person with a sensible friend who, when asked, "What did they say about me?" will reply, "Nothing," rather than, "That you're a jerk."

Gossip has its promoters. "If you can't say anything good about someone, sit right here by me," said Alice Roosevelt Longworth, Teddy's daughter.

Yet before you dissect someone's personality, be aware that if you trash others, you, too, are probably getting talked about. "If you scatter thorns," goes the Italian proverb, "don't go barefoot."

To be honest, honesty itself can be overrated. For example, if a friend says, "Do you like this song I just wrote?" rather than make a gagging gesture, just say, "I like your last one better," and explain why. Honesty counts, but so does tact and staying aware of other people's feelings.

In the words of singer Joni Mitchell: "There are things to confess that enrich the world and things that need not be said."

Words can hurt.

You never saw a fish on the wall with its mouth shut.

—Sally Berger

I'm great at keeping secrets. (My husband is terrible at it. Never tell him anything.) But even I have been known to *occasionally* whisper, "Don't tell that I told you, but . . ."

Be realistic. If you can't keep your mouth shut, can you really expect others to zip theirs?

Some secrets should be told (for example, if someone abuses you, tell an adult you trust). And sometimes you need a second opinion. But once you put words in the airwaves, you cannot press Delete or say, "Kidding!" (Even if you press Unsend on AOL it can be a moment too late.)

Try not to play telephone with your own or a friend's intimate news. If you're burning to unload, tell a faraway cousin or an out-of-school friend.

Wait, you think your friends Aaron and Erin have a right to know that someone said he's a dweeb and that she over-tweezes her eyebrows? Think again. If you spill all, you're not being a good reporter, you're being insensitive. And both the dissees and the disser may wish you'd kept quiet.

Trust me, people really do *not* need to hear all about Lulu's luau if they didn't get invited. You don't have to lie about it; just don't volunteer that Saturday's party was the best you've ever been to.

Not everything that pops into your head should leap from your lips.

The trouble with reputation is that you either
haven't enough of it or you have entirely too much.
Procton Churdge

I hope rumors never get spread about you. But if it happens, don't freak. People do not believe everything they hear, and even awful rumors blow right over.

You want to publicly deny a comment? Okay. But don't shout, "I never kissed her!" or "I am not bulimic!" or "We didn't do it," as this may keep morons murmuring. And don't e-mail your class to set the record straight because your message can get forwarded far and wide, which will keep the conversation alive much longer than necessary.

You're best off saying quietly and firmly, "You know that's not true." If you can manage to sound calm even though you're in a blind rage, your words will have weight, and the rumor will fade away fast. (Rumor? What rumor?)

Are people talking about your friends? Don't stand back saying nothing when your friends could use a show of loyalty. Defend them. Say, "He's shy, but he's a good guy," or "If you got to know her, you'd like her."

Stick up for friends, and they'll stick up for you. "Do not protect yourself by a fence," a Czech proverb goes, "but rather by your friends."

Nobody serious takes rumors seriously.

Anything you can do, I can do better.

—IRVING BERLIN

Sometimes, even the best of friends become jealous of each other. I envied one girl because she had a big fat clothes allowance whereas I had to be a cashier and round-the-clock baby-sitter to get my spending money. I was jealous of another because she was off-the-charts beautiful and the guys *I* noticed noticed *her.*

If you ever find yourself envying a friend, try not to let it poison your relationship. If you envy a friend's grades, work to bring up your own. If you envy a friend's ability to spike a volleyball, practice your spiking. And accept that while you can't do everything, you, too, have special skills and good fortunes. Some people—maybe even your friends—probably envy *you.* (If you know a friend envies you, try to boost that person up by pointing out and complimenting his/her strengths and qualities.)

An old Flemish proverb says: "I may envy your shoes . . . but do they pinch your feet?" We all have lucky and less lucky parts of our lives, and no one knows what really goes on inside a particular mansion or shack. Just because someone's life *looks* perfect does not mean it is.

I have a few friends who are rich or famous. Do I envy them? No. Call me a mushball, but what sometimes gets to me now is when I'm at an airport, and I see a daughter get off a plane and give her father a big, long, wonderful bear hug. My dad died a long time ago, so I can't do that anymore. Those are people I sometimes briefly envy.

The more content you are, the less vulnerable to envy.

"What it begins with, I know finally, is the kernel of meanness in people's hearts," wrote novelist Jane Hamilton.

We all have a little piece of us that is jealous, mean, or petty. But most of us have that kernel under control. If we're angry or sulking and the urge to phone someone and scream at 3:00 A.M. wells up, we squelch it and go back to sleep, partly because the person may have Caller ID, but also because we know we may regret in the morning whatever was said in the middle of the night.

Of course, some people let their mean streaks take over. They're the vicious, sullen bullies other people fear.

I've got news for you. Bullies are unhappy. After all, when you feel good, you *don't* put effort into making others feel bad.

"When people pick on you," said Kelly Rowland of Destiny's Child, "it's usually because you have something they don't have."

Should you stay out of their way? Sure. But rather than hating or fearing them, consider feeling sorry for them. Don't say, "You're an insecure loser and I feel sorry for you!" Just think it quietly. This puts you in the power position and lets their behavior be their problem, not yours.

"I will permit no man to narrow and degrade my soul by making me hate him," wrote educator Booker T. Washington.

Mean often means miserable.

The law 'an eye for an eye' leaves everyone blind.

—martin Luther King Jr.

D o you really want to fight?

Why not call a truce? Or say, "Forget it, I don't want to fight over this"? How about apologizing? Not a lame "I'm sorry if what I said ticked you off" but a heartfelt "I'm sorry, really."

World champion fighter Muhammad Ali said, "You know, I hate fighting. If I knew how to make a living some other way, I would."

Charlotte Brontë, who wrote *Jane Eyre*, said, "Life appears to me too short to be spent in nursing animosity or registering wrongs."

Let peace prevail. Prevent quarrels from escalating into battles. When someone tries to smear his/her bad mood all over everyone else, try not to let that person's problem become your problem. When someone wants to fight, stay calm and walk away.

Note: While tattling is a risky business, if you ever feel honest-to-God afraid, go ahead and speak to an adult you trust. When you need help, it's brave, not cowardly, to ask for it.

Put down your dukes.

Being angry with people hurts you more than it hurts them.

—OPRAH WINFREY

D o you hold grudges for months on end? Why? You're just letting the person continue to hurt you—and that's giving him or her too much power.

Getting mad at someone who has been unreasonable may be reasonable, but it's still a brain drain. So try to lengthen your fuse. And when you're mad, try to rectify things. If it's a close friend (or parent or teacher), try to talk it out (talk, not yell). Use "I" statements: Say, "*I* got upset when . . ." not "How could *you* have done that . . . ?" Be specific: Say, "Want to come over Sunday afternoon?" not "You never come over anymore!"

If it's someone you hardly know, and there's no easy solution in sight, just let it go. If it's a friend who keeps letting you down, let him or her go.

Eleanor Roosevelt said: "If someone betrays you once, it is his fault; if he betrays you twice, it is your fault."

When you're angry, you could get all pinched up and plot revenge and waste *your* time obsessing. Or you could take a walk, watch a comedy, call a friend, play a game, write a letter you will never send, or go outside with a dog and a stick. It might also help to talk to a shrink. Try, really try, to flick your anger away rather than letting it build and fester.

Eleanor Roosevelt also said this: "Anger is only one letter short of danger."

Let go of anger.

He has the right to criticize who has the heart to help.

—abraham Lincoln

You wouldn't hang out with someone who was constantly saying, "Hurry! You're so slow!" or "Is that the best you can draw?" or "Where'd you get *that*? The Salvation Army?"

No one likes to be criticized. So if you and your friends have gotten into a habit of laughing not with but *at* one another, it's time to break the pattern.

Ask yourself, "Is it worth opening my mouth to say *that*?" Remember that dissers get dissed, whereas complimenters tend to get complimented.

Even if you are being critical with good intentions, express yourself carefully. Don't say, "How can you not get this? It's so easy!" Say, "Want me to explain logarithms?" Don't say, "Stop whining about your weight and start doing something about it!" Say, "You want exercise? Let's go for a run." Don't say, "You suck at pitching." Say, "Let me show you what the coach showed me."

The world can be heartless. Friends shouldn't be.

Happy is the house that shelters a friend!
—ralph waldo emerson

re you a good guest? The kind who gets invited back? If you are
planning to spend a long weekend at a friend's house . . .

★ Give them a gift—flowers or food—or take photos of their family to send afterward with a note of thanks.

★ Be easygoing. If the family suggests watching a foreign movie, don't say you hate subtitles. (Besides, have you seen *Crouching Tiger, Hidden Dragon,* or these Italian movies: *Life Is Beautiful, Cinema Paradiso,* or *Il Postino*?)

★ Allow the friend and family some quiet time. Take a book.

★ Try not to be a picky eater.

★ Say, "Please," and "Thanks," and "Delicious!" and offer to help with dishes.

★ Charm your friend's little siblings. The kids will appreciate it and so will the parents.

★ Speaking of friends' parents, call them something. Use their first or last names, but don't just slink past. (And when you see them in a store, don't act as if they don't look familiar. Say hi.)

★ Rinse the sink after brushing your teeth. Use tissues, not towels, for shaving cuts or makeup. And flush. (Hey, some people need reminding.)

★ Do not overstay your welcome. Know when to say thank you and good-bye. (You don't like being in host mode forever, right?)

★ Dash off a quick thank-you note. (Warning: The longer you wait, the better it should be.)

Great guests get invited to great places.

He hath eaten me out of house and home,

he hath put all my substance into that fat belly of his.

—WILLIAM SHAKESPEARE

It's one thing to be a good guest—another to be a mega mooch who uses a friend for his or her car or horse or swimming pool or stocked refrigerator or famous parent.

No one likes to be used.

Money and friendship are also a bad mix. Yes, your friend enjoys going bowling with you. But not if you *never* pay for yourself. Yes, your friend likes arcade games. But not if you always forget your wallet at home. Even if one friend has much more money than the other, it's still nice if the treating goes both ways.

So enjoy your friends. But don't mistake them for banks, stables, pool clubs, grocery stores, or employment offices. Don't take advantage of them or they may start resenting you.

Friendships should be give-and-take. Not take-and-take. Not give-and-give. Try to get the balance right.

If you use your friends, you'll lose your friends.

Crick said it wasn't his fault that every place he went,
he met up with people who made him do bad things.

Yeah, well, Crick's still the one who ends up in jail in that novel. We *are* responsible for our own actions. And some friends are trouble. Do yours pull you down?

If you ride a motorcycle with a beer in your hand and no helmet on your head, you'll break bones. If your gang gets into street fights, you'll get beaten up. If you all start smoking, you'll wreck your health. If you're into drugs, you might wind up in jail or worse. If you drink and keep drinking, your real life might slip away from you.

If your circle of friends is not the circle you want for yourself, move toward friends you'd rather have. Get involved in new activities, in school or out. Call someone and issue a specific invitation, such as, "Want to go hiking on Saturday?" rather than a vague one such as, "Want to do something some time?"

You *can* shake up your social life. New friends are out there—and you can find them.

"Louis," said Rick at the end of *Casablanca,* "I think this is the beginning of a beautiful friendship."

Find friends who bring out your best.

relationships

mindbodyfriendsrelationshipsschoolfamilyworkquotesadvice

The course of true love never did run smooth.

—WILLIAM SHAKESPEARE

No one ever said it was easy.

According to James Baldwin, "Love is a battle, love is a war; love is a growing up."

According to Pablo Picasso, "Love is the greatest refreshment of life."

According to François de la Rochefoucauld, "True love is like ghosts that everyone talks about and few have seen."

And you? What's your take on love?

Love is complicated.

I don't have a love life. I have a like life.

—lorrie moore

In *War and Peace*, Russian novelist Leo Tolstoy wrote, "She felt sorry for herself: sorry that she was being wasted all this time and of no use to anyone—while she herself felt so capable of loving and being loved."

It *is* hard to be patient. Always has been. It was for Tolstoy's character Natasha, and it was for me, and I bet it is for you.

People used to stare at phones waiting for a ring. Now they sometimes stare at computer screens waiting for a ping.

Many people imagine that they are the only person in the grade who hasn't yet gone out with anyone. Not true. If you list the names of all the girls or guys in your class and try to write the name of a boyfriend or girlfriend by each, you'll see that most people have not paired off. It just seems that way because lovey-dovey couples are extra visible.

Love takes time. And some individuals are more ready for romance than others. If you've fallen for a person who is making booger jokes, obsessed with cat stickers, or holding burping contests, don't take it personally if said crush is unaware of your existence. But do check back in a year or two.

While you can't make someone sign up for a relationship, before you know it, girls and guys really do grow up and find each other.

All in good time.

If you find your soul mate, it's because you've
figured out what your own soul is.

Sandra Bullock

H ow well do you know yourself?

"Love yourself first and everything else falls into line," said actress Lucille Ball.

"Not to idolize myself or anything like that, but I'm a big fan of me," said *Saturday Night Live*'s Jimmy Fallon.

You aren't drawn to people who act needy or cranky, or who spend their hours stuck to a sofa, are you? Well, guess what? The love of your life will find you faster if you are not inside giving off negative vibes but outside having fun and being part of the world.

Do your crushes say, "I'm such a loser" or "No one would ever like me"? No. So don't bad-mouth yourself. Work on finding your best self and being the kind of person you like to hang out with. Join the band, yearbook committee, chess club, or a sport you love. It's often when you're happily involved in a group situation that you'll meet an individual you might want to know better. And who might want to know *you* better.

Care about yourself before caring about someone else.

Love, and you shall be loved.
—ralph waldo emerson

Unfortunately, there's no guarantee that the person you like will like you back and there's no way to force the issue. On the other hand, if you keep your feelings completely to yourself, your chances of sparking a romance are next to nil.

So get out there and smile, say hi, meet the person's eyes, show interest, and ask questions. Your chances of establishing a relationship will go up. Way up.

That's how it works: Be a giving, caring, loving sort of person, and others start giving, caring, and loving back. People also approach and pay attention to those who approach and pay attention to them.

"Love requires boldness and scorns bashfulness," said British author Thomas Fuller.

Be lovable. Give romance a chance. After all, it's a shame when an older man and woman see each other at a high school reunion and confess, decades too late, that they both had secret feelings for each other. As poet John Greenleaf Whittier wrote,

For all sad words of tongue or pen,
The saddest are these: "It might have been."

Love isn't just a noun. It's also a verb.

I was always the girl who had a crush on a guy who didn't want me.

−tyra Banks

The best way to be lucky in love is to take your time and choose carefully.

Many people forget this. Instead of noticing someone on their own, they go for the person everyone else is going for. In school, do almost all the girls like one or two particular guys, while almost all the guys like one or two girls?

If so, do the math.

It's not that you don't deserve a superstar's devotion. I'm sure you're every bit as amazing as that handful of gods/goddesses with mass appeal. But since everyone else is hitting on them, your chances of being plucked from the crowd are slim. Who needs it?

What would happen if you bypassed the group choice and discovered someone undiscovered? What if you joked with the student editor who prints your movie reviews? Smiled back at the exchange student with the cute accent? Sent a fun unexpected e-mail? Looked more closely at your lab partner? What if you asked the computer genius or piano prodigy for one-on-one help? How could it hurt?

Rather than pine for a crowd-pleaser, zero in on a worthy yet overlooked hottie who shares your interests and may respond to some attention. You could be heading toward a two-way relationship instead of staying in a one-way rut.

Charles Schulz pointed out in *Peanuts*: "Nothing spoils the taste of peanut butter like unrequited love." True. But remind yourself that if the person you zero in on doesn't zero in on you, you *will* survive. You will! Always hold on to that thought—just in case.

Why choose someone who isn't choosing you?

When love is not madness, it is not love.

—Pedro Calderón de la Barca

"Love would not be love if it did not slip over into the excessive," wrote novelist Edna O'Brien.

"The measure of love is to love without measure," wrote Saint Augustine.

Maybe so, but here's the rub: Loving madly, excessively, and without measure can be risky and depressing if your beloved is not deserving or does not love you back.

Nevertheless, many people don't just *like* their crush, they *luv luuvv luuuvvv* him or her. They place the individual high up on a pedestal and admire from way down below. They become obsessed. In extreme cases, they moan that they would die for him or her.

This isn't love (which is never totally sensible). It's infatuation (which is often totally nuts).

Question: Are you in love with love, or are you really in love with Jamie, Alex, Casey, or Sam? (Note the cleverly picked unisex names.) Try to care about the person, not your romantic notion of the person. And try not to become so crazy about your crush that you leave the crush no choice but to disappoint you by tumbling off the pedestal. (Once you're on a pedestal, there's only one way to go.)

You aren't perfect; neither is your crush. And if you actually get to know your Fantasy Person, you may find that here on Earth, he or she is not as worthy and wondrous as you thought. (Better to find out sooner than later.) Or you may find that you two don't have much in common. (Sigh.) Or, who knows? You may find that you connect in an amazing way—imperfections and all. (Yay!)

Stepping into love beats falling on your face.

GIRLS,
SKIP THE NEXT PAGE.
THIS INFO IS FOR
GUYS ONLY!

He knew she was there by the joy and fear that
overwhelmed his heart.

—LEO tOLStOY

Hey, guys, if you're wondering, *How can I tell her I like her and how can I tell if she likes me?* here's my advice: Don't *tell* her, *show* her. Don't ask point blank because if, God forbid, she does not like you back, you've gone public with private feelings and gotten your ego shredded for nothing.

So how *do* you show her you like her? Smile, say hi, ask about stuff she cares about, laugh at her jokes, compliment her, make eye contact, sit near her, use her name when talking to her, call, e-mail, and don't be afraid to act happy that she's around. You don't want to come on tooooo strong, but you want to let her know that if she puts down her lunch tray next to yours, you won't leave—you'll smile.

Okay. Now how can you tell if *she* likes you back? Notice her behavior in return. Some girls flirt with everybody, so it's hard to be sure when they like a particular guy. Others are shy even when their hearts are pounding. As Edward Albee said, "What's true and what isn't is a tricky business, no?" Usually, though, when a girl likes you, she looks at you, smiles, says hi, compliments you, laughs at your jokes, e-mails back, calls, and pays lots of attention to you.

It's happening? Excellent! Enjoy her company. Or go ahead and ask her out.

Uh-oh. You're sending I-like-you signals, but getting *none* back? Hang on to your pride, and move on. There are m-i-l-l-i-o-n-s of other girls.

Signals: Send them clearly; read them carefully.

GUYS,
SKIP THE NEXT PAGE.
THIS INFO IS FOR
GIRLS ONLY!

I don't want to be wise, ever, Mama, ever. I'm in love.
—LILLIAN HELLMAN

Pssst, girls, if you're wondering, *How can I tell him I like him and how can I tell if he likes me?* here's my advice: Don't *tell* him, *show* him. Don't ask point blank because if, God forbid, he does not like you back, you've gone public with private feelings and gotten your ego shredded for nothing.

So how *do* you show him you like him? Smile, say hi, ask about stuff he cares about, laugh at his jokes, compliment him, make eye contact, sit near him, use his name when talking to him, call, e-mail, and don't be afraid to act happy that he's around. You don't want to come on tooooo strong, but you want to let him know that if he puts down his lunch tray next to yours, you won't leave—you'll smile.

Okay. Now how can you tell if *he* likes you back? Notice his behavior in return. Some guys flirt with everybody, so it's hard to be sure when they like a particular girl. Others are shy even when their hearts are pounding. As Edward Albee said, "What's true and what isn't is a tricky business, no?" Usually, though, when a guy likes you, he looks at you, smiles, says hi, compliments you, laughs at your jokes, e-mails back, calls, and pays lots of attention to you.

It's happening? Excellent! Enjoy his company. Or go ahead and ask him out.

Uh-oh. You're sending I-like-you signals, but getting *none* back? Hang on to your pride, and move on. There are m-i-l-l-i-o-n-s of other guys.

Signals: Send them clearly; read them carefully.

Love enters a man through his eyes; a woman through her ears.
—POLISH PROVERB

Did you read both the guys' and girls' pages? Thought so! Girls and guys are not thaaaaat different after all! Having or not having Y chromosomes does not dictate every aspect of a person's behavior—nor should it.

What about the above proverb? Is it true? Sexist? Both?

One hates to generalize, and this page may get me in trouble, but many young guys (I said "many" not "all") do have a knee-jerk habit of instantly checking out girls. Girls check out guys, too, but many (there's that "many") take a few extra seconds to notice which guys, the cute and less cute, have something to say and a nice way of saying it. Another difference? Well, Conan O'Brien said, "A study in the *Washington Post* says that women have better verbal skills than men. I just want to say to the authors of that study: Duh."

What's to learn here? Probably that *both* guys and girls should keep their eyes and ears open, and stay aware of how they look and sound.

Mind you, if someone is interested in you only because of how you look, think twice about being interested back.

Another stereotype is that girls sometimes (note the "sometimes") look for long-term relationships whereas guys look for short-term fireworks. As Cervantes's Don Quixote put it: "Love in young men, for the most part, is not love at all but simply sexual desire, and its accomplishment is its end." I don't agree 100 percent with the Man of La Mancha, but do be careful. You don't want to get hurt and you don't want to hurt anyone else.

Use your eyes, ears, and common sense.

If you do not tell the truth about yourself,
you cannot tell it about other people.

—Virginia Woolf

Do you have any friends who would never speak directly to their own crushes, but who are all too eager to report your feelings to the person you care about? Beware!

Sometimes it's useful when one person reveals that a third person has you on the brain. Go-betweens can help jump-start new relationships or patch up faltering ones. That's what the Beatles' song "She Loves You" is about.

But third parties can often be troublemakers. They can mangle messages or go after your crush themselves. They can make your beloved self-conscious and uncomfortable. And you should never fully rely on third parties—or be one.

Get to know your crush—don't just send out spies and messengers.

Think for yourself—don't go out with someone because you hear that person likes you, or break up because you hear that person's feelings have changed.

One-on-one time is what launches real relationships and keeps them going.

Do it yourself.

Judge not the horse by its saddle.

—CHINESE PROVERB

Y ou'd never judge people solely by how much money they (or their parents) have, would you? Or by their clothes or homes or cars? It's better to get to know them!

"Being with a guy just because he's rich," said Candace Bushnell, who created the show *Sex and the City*, "seems like a good idea until you actually try it. And then you're, like, 'I don't care if I eat Campbell's soup for the rest of my life.'"

Money is handy. But there's a saying that if you marry for money, you'll earn every penny. And that goes for brides *and* grooms.

Never assume you know what someone is really worth.

Love is a great beautifier.

—Louisa May Alcott

S trange things can happen once you get to know someone. People you hardly noticed can gradually—or suddenly—become cuter and more fascinating.

Ever see *Beauty and the Beast*? Remember when Belle runs away and the Beast saves her from the wolves? She tends to his scratches and sings, "True, he is no Prince Charming, but there's something in him that I simply didn't see." Next thing you know, the wardrobe, candelabra, and teapot all join in a rousing chorus of "There may be something there that wasn't there before."

I like that scene. And I know from personal experience that feelings can and do change. Today's buddy can become tomorrow's crush or sweetheart. A person who isn't even on your radar screen can morph into someone who becomes front and center and very, very visible.

Look again.

Everybody complains about the weather but nobody
does anything about it.

−mark twain

Talking about the weather may seem like a lame way to start a conversation, but it's better than standing around saying nothing at all. Try, "It's a beautiful day—I wish we were outside." Or "I can't believe it's raining again."

If you can talk to your friends, you can talk to the person who makes you happy-nervous.

Other tried-and-true icebreakers? Ask what time it is. Give a compliment. Ask about a movie or last night's TV show or homework or weekend plans.

During school, talk about the here and now. "How was history?" "Did you read the chapter?" "What was the assignment?" "Are you going to the game?" "Can you show me how to do this?"

During a dance, say, "I like this song," or "They really changed the gym," or "This is a good party, isn't it?" Feeling bold? Try, "You have a nice smile," or "You dance so well," or "That sweater matches your eyes."

When possible, get beyond small talk. "I have come to believe," said poet Audre Lorde, "that what is most important to me must be spoken, made verbal and shared, even at the risk of having it bruised or misunderstood."

By the way, it's also okay just to sway together quietly. As Greek historian Plutarch said, "Silence at the proper season is wisdom and better than any speech."

Break the ice.

Love that has not friendship for its base is like
a mansion built upon the sand.
—ella WHeeLer WILCOX

E ver had a crush on a friend? If you declare your devotion and are met with, "Really? Um, I'm flattered, but I like you as a friend," your friendship might go through an awkward phase—or possibly slide down the tubes. So hold your cards closer to your chest as you attempt to gauge the person's interest. Look in his/her eyes and notice if those baby blues (browns, greens, or hazels) gaze back. Touch the person lightly on the arm, and see if there is a shift toward you—or away. Dress up a little; suggest taking a walk; use the person's name—e.g., "David, that is so funny!" or "Pretty earrings, Olivia." Test the waters before jumping in.

If you're brazen, consider saying, "I heard a crazy rumor that we were going out. Can you imagine?" Notice if the person (a) gags or (b) turns purple or (c) smiles and says, "Not so crazy—I have a good imagination," thereby lobbing the ball back in your court.

Miracles do happen. Friendships do blossom and evolve and sometimes catch fire. In the movie *Broadcast News,* Aaron Altman said, "I would give anything if you were two people so that I could call up the one who's my friend and tell her about the one that I like so much."

But miracles are rare. So if your friend-crush keeps blathering on about his/her crush on *someone else,* take heart. Sparkling friendship often outlasts fragile romance, and guy-girl friendships are wonderful in their own right. Besides, if you wait awhile, someday your friend might see you in a new light—or *you* might wonder how you ever considered those lips kissable.

Friendship into love? Proceed with caution.

I now understand, at long last, that in a great relationship,
you can still maintain all the things that make you happy.
I think a lot of my misunderstanding of relationships was in thinking
I had to evaporate to be someone's girlfriend.

—Julia Roberts

Y ou're not supposed to be someone else's mirror or cheerleader or sidekick. You're supposed to be the same complex and compelling person that your boyfriend or girlfriend fell for in the first place.

If you give up all the things that make you *you,* watch out. You may end up resenting your sweetheart, and he/she may end up losing interest. You love soccer and he loves football? Fine. Attend each other's games when possible, but don't give up your own sport. You have friends and so does she? Great. Do some things as a group, but keep seeing friends one-on-one, too.

You have a brain and a personality and a life of your own. Don't change them or ditch your friends just because you're going out with someone. Don't evaporate.

"And stand together yet not too near together," advised Kahlil Gibran. "For the pillars of the temple stand apart, and the oak tree and the cypress grow not in each other's shadow."

Hold on to yourself.

Human love is often but the encounter
of two weaknesses.
—François mauriac

I f you two come together because you're both lonely and needy and desperate to kiss someone (anyone! ANYONE!!, **ANYONE!!!**), your relationship probably won't last long.

But if you get along, care about each other, root for each other, and enjoy each other's strengths while also accepting each other's short-comings, you just may have something there.

Be open, not desperate.

It's hard for me to truly connect with people.

So when it clicks, it's amazing.

—Kirsten Dunst

If the person you've been noticing starts noticing you back, be sure to notice!

Has your crush been blushing or stammering or asking about you or showing up where you happen to be? Hurray! Have you been cornering each other at parties? This is *not* coincidence. Do you call each other by nicknames? When you talk, do you feel suddenly shy—or like you could talk forever? Do you compliment each other? Are you swapping e-mails? When you said, "That's a great color on you!" did your crush start wearing forest green day after day after day? These are all good signs!

In P. L. Travers's *Mary Poppins*, when Bert shouted, "Mary!" in a way that showed she "was a very important person in his life," Mary looked down at her feet and tapped her shoe. "Then she smiled at the shoe in such a way that the shoe knew quite well that the smile wasn't meant for it."

Are you reading each other's smiles? Are things beginning to click? If so, rejoice! Be brave and recognize the flirting for what it is! (But you still don't have to rush to label it.)

When things are moving in the right direction . . . enjoy!

What a lovely surprise to discover how un-lonely

being alone can be.

—ELLEN BURSTYN

I know this is the Relationships chapter. But I want to put in a word (or 262 words) about being single. It's fine to be single! Beats going out with lowlifes or feeling like a vulnerable kid on an endless roller-coaster ride.

Some people aren't up for the whole relationship thing. They'd rather focus on friends, sports, homework. They like being able to do whatever they want, whenever they want. They like being independent and able to flirt. They like having their options open, time free, and possibilities endless.

No problem there.

Others jump from one love tangle to another and never take a moment to figure out who they really are and what they really want.

And that, my friend, *can* be a problem.

It's nice to be in love. But don't be afraid to be alone. Being alone doesn't mean you're unattractive, any more than being part of a couple means you are attractive. And there's something kind of nice about *not* having your Friday nights all booked up. Besides, going out with one person can sometimes be limiting and can lead to quarrels, jealousy, pressure, or hurt feelings. Alone and unattached, you get to make your own schedule and keep yourself company. And who's better company than you?

"Inside myself is a place where I live all alone," wrote novelist Pearl S. Buck, who won the Nobel Prize. "I never found the companion as companionable as solitude," said Henry David Thoreau.

Alone, yes. Lonely, no.

Someone's sexuality does not define their essence.

—rosie o'donnell

A nother clarification: This chapter has been addressing girls who like guys and guys who like girls, but it's okay to rearrange any pronouns. In other words, if you are a girl who is attracted to girls, or a guy who is attracted to guys, please know that you are not the only one, and all this relationship advice still applies. Love is love no matter the couple.

You may know for sure that you're straight. Or gay. Or perhaps you are confused about all this. For many, sexual orientation takes time to sort out. Keep getting to know yourself rather than hurrying to define yourself.

If you are a girl who has noticed the beauty of other girls, or a guy who has noticed the appeal of other guys, this does not necessarily mean you are gay. This means you have eyes. If, however, all your crushes are on members of your own sex, this may indicate that your sexual orientation is something to keep thinking about.

The more comfortable and self-accepting you are, the more comfortable and accepting your friends and family will be.

If you are in middle school and are pretty sure you are gay, should you "come out"? Maybe. But I wouldn't necessarily rush it. Your community may not be as broad-minded and supportive as you'd like, and the advantage of living more openly may be offset by other people's misconceptions and whisperings. Fortunately, by high school and college, not only is it easier to join groups in which gay students can meet and talk, but many more straight peers will have come to realize that we aren't all mirrors of one another, and that this is absolutely okay.

Love? Love is normal.

It's delightful, it's delicious, it's de-lovely.

—COLE PORTER

When you love someone and that person loves you back, it's pretty great. You feel energized, understood, cherished, and generous.

So if you're actually going out with someone, don't just analyze the relationship and fret about its future. Revel in the present. Be smart and responsible, yes. But have fun. Smile like crazy inside.

"It is a poor heart that never rejoices," wrote Charles Dickens.

"Love is the heartbeat of all life," wrote Paramahansa Yogananda.

Impressionist painter Paul Gauguin said, *"Soyez amoureuse et soyez heureuse,"* which, for those of you not taking *français* means, "Be in love and be happy."

Are you in love? Are you happy? Newbery medalist E. L. Konigsburg said, "Happiness is excitement that has found a settling down place, but there is always a little corner that keeps flapping around."

Live a little. Love a little.

Love is lovely.

The only true language in the world is a kiss.
—alfred de musset

O h, those French!

Is a kiss a language? Hmm. Different kisses certainly have different meanings.

There are delightful kisses. "A kiss is a lovely trick designed by nature to stop speech when words become superfluous," said Ingrid Bergman.

And deceitful ones. "What lies lurk in kisses," observed Heinrick Heine.

There's wild romantic rapture. "O love! O fire! Once he drew with one long kiss, my whole soul through my lips," wrote Alfred, Lord Tennyson.

And sterile perfunctory pecks. Steve Martin described a "kiss that was so formal, it might as well have been wearing a tuxedo."

There's meaningful making-out, and there are kisses so casual, they're weightless. Maybe kissing is a language—a romance language that is fun to learn, but tricky to translate.

Finally, let me quote Jonathan Swift, who mused long ago, "I wonder what fool it was that first invented kissing."

Fool? Genius?

Kisses count.

Then come kiss me, sweet and twenty,

youth's a stuff will not endure.

—WILLIaM SHaKeSPeare

Kisses mean more when you care about the person attached to the lips. If you two have been going out for a while (five days is *not* a while) and you've been holding hands and nuzzling but haven't quite kissed, it's going to be wonderful when you do.

If however, you're playing Spin the Bottle or Truth or Dare, and you and someone you barely know are suddenly in a dark closet mashing mouths, it won't be the same. It just won't. Trust me.

Are you worried the other person might kiss and tell? He or she might. As Joan Rivers quipped, "Anyone who believes that only time will tell hasn't been in a boys' locker room."

What if you haven't kissed anybody yet? Relax. Everyone has a first time, and the person you are about to kiss might be new at it, too, or consider it an honor to share your first kiss. ("Surely it is a great day for every girl when she receives her first kiss," Anne Frank confided to her diary.)

As for P.D.A. (public displays of affection), making out is not a spectator sport. It can be fun to kiss at amusement parks or movies, but why stage a make-out session by your locker or at your parents' party or in front of a sad, lovelorn friend who is getting over a breakup?

Kisses—make them sweet, not sour.

When I was in high school, I was the captain of the Virginity Team. My mother was the coach. I don't know why we had cheerleaders because no one ever scored.

—caroline rhea

Kisses—from formal to French—are one thing, but if you get too physical too soon, you're running real risks.

What risks? Well, in no particular order: getting your heart broken, getting a reputation (fair or not), getting a disease (curable or *incurable*), and getting pregnant.

Note: No matter how cute you think babies are, you honestly don't want one yet. Babies require care 24/7; they go through thousands of diapers; and before you know it they aren't chubby little infants anymore, they are demanding preschoolers in need of food, shoes, and a decent education. One decade later, and they are teens capable of turning you into a grandparent!

"I have a lot of friends who really messed their lives up," said Justin Timberlake. "They're teenagers and they already have children just because they couldn't keep it zipped. That's just stupid, right?"

You don't want to start another life.

You also don't want to shorten your own. "It's the lives of young people that are put at risk by unsafe sex," said Colin Powell. "Therefore, protect yourself."

Millions of teenagers already have sexually transmitted diseases. Many do not even know it yet and are not getting the treatment they need.

So be caring, but be careful. And remember that love isn't really about touching someone—it's about reaching someone.

Slow down. You're better off waiting.

I really hate the thought of being intimate with
somebody and then it's over.
—mariah carey

Sex is compleX and rated X, and most students are not "doing it." It may seem that way since couples who paw each other in the hallways stand out more than students who meander to class. Hooking up is a vague term that means different things to different people, but make no mistake: Virgins are the silent majority. Most kids are not as experienced as they might like you to believe.

Besides, savvy couples know they can have a lot of fun without running major risks and spending the next weeks, months, or years worrying about or regretting the consequences of being together.

If you *are* being intimate with someone, are you absolutely sure you both want to be going as far as you're going? Are you doing what you both want to be doing? Is all of this working for both of you? Sex should never be about one person pressuring or taking advantage of another person. If you don't want to do something (or are not ready to do something), don't do it. (And if you *are*, use protection!)

By the way, if you aren't positive that you are secure enough to say, "I don't want to," or that the other person isn't caring enough to hear you, then avoid backseats and lights-out situations. Why get physically close to someone you can't really talk to?

Sex should not be a one-way street.

For many years, I shut down that place inside myself
that needed to rage, cry, ask questions.
—tori amos

W hile I'm waving the Be Careful banner, let me very briefly address date rape. Date rape is when one person wants to have sex and the other person does not, but the first person does not respect the second person's wishes.

This is a crime, a tragedy, and more common than it should be.

Guys—and I know most of you know this—listen to the woman you're with. If she says no, don't hear yes. If you force yourself on someone, that's not love, that's violence, and you can be prosecuted.

Girls, if you don't know your date all that well, don't just assume he is trustworthy. Don't act supersexy, get drunk, and go off alone with a man if he has no idea that you're going to want to put on the brakes. Be clear about what's okay and what is not so you can avoid misunderstanding or disaster.

On the other hand, please know that if you *have* been molested or sexually abused, what happened was not your fault. Just as a child who is molested was innocent, a teen or an adult who is raped is not to blame. The abuser is at fault, not the victim.

"Rape is the only crime in which the victim becomes the accused," wrote Freda Adler.

"I made a conscious choice," said Tori Amos, singer, songwriter, and rape survivor, "not to stay a victim anymore."

Play it safe.

If you really love somebody, nothing can get in the way.

—JUSTIN TIMBERLAKE

I have these really great teenage cousins who read this chapter while it was still a bunch of typed-up pages. They offered helpful comments, and I said I'd thank them in the Acknowledgments.

But was that enough for them? Noooooo! They said (and I paraphrase), "You quote Shakespeare and Timberlake; why can't you quote us?" and they came up with this Pet Peeves page. According to my extended family, Justin is off the mark because tons of things can get in the way of love. Not just age, parents, and distance, but other stuff, too.

For instance, it's a major turnoff when:

Anna Ausubel: ". . . people constantly put themselves down."

Matt Bird: ". . . people don't shower, wash their hair, or brush their teeth."

Sarah Jeffrey: ". . . people try to change their personality just to gain status."

Elizabeth Ackerman: ". . . the person you like always completes your sentences."

Robbie Jeffrey: ". . . someone wants you to be someone you're not."

Johnny Ausubel: ". . . the person you like is locked in a group of friends so there's no way to even say hello."

Emme Ackerman: ". . . you trust someone with a secret and then he jokes about it."

Stephanie May: ". . . people let their opinions get warped by what their friends think."

Don't shoot love in the foot. It's hard enough to get a relationship going.

Get out of the way and give love a chance.

I like not only to be loved but also to be told that I am loved.
—george eliot

A journalist asked playwright Tom Stoppard if there's a better way to say "I love you." He replied, "No, simplicity is good. Subject, verb, object."

Still, take your time before saying "I love you." Why? Because the sentence may be simple, but its meaning is immense. It's unfair to say you love someone who loves you if you really aren't as serious. And if you say "I love you" to a toad or toadette who dumps you next Tuesday, you'll feel even more stepped on than if you had not labeled your feelings.

When you really love someone, you have a back-and-forth, give-and-take connection and you can laugh together and talk about troubles and think out loud. You like hanging out in private or in public. You look forward to seeing and talking to each other and you miss each other when apart. When together, you don't feel self-conscious or pressured, but secure, calm, at peace. Your bond is real—not obsessive or one-way or all in your head.

Once you've said, "I love you," it's impossible to take those three words back. So be sure it's a long-lasting love—not a fleeting romance, not a fantasy. Give your feelings time to grow and deepen.

By the way, if you want, you can say something like, "I love spending time with you," or "I love talking with you." These are powerful phrases, but unlike "I love you," they won't land you all the way out on a limb or require a timely soul-searching response.

Little words, large impact.

When I give, I give myself.

—Walt Whitman

Some couples get bent out of shape trying to decide what to give each other. But the nicest gifts aren't the most expensive, they're the ones that show you were thinking about each other. You didn't bake her *your* favorite cake (chocolate)—you baked *her* favorite (lemon).You didn't get him *your* favorite CD—you got one you thought *he'd* like. Whether your gift is a stuffed animal, framed photo, or book, a gift that shows forethought beats a gift that shows you dashed into the nearest convenience store.

Time and attention and caring, not stuff from shelves, is, of course, the best gift of all. "Love," said John Lennon, "is like a precious plant. You've got to keep watering it, really look after it, and nurture it."

Or how about a homemade present? If you can draw a portrait, sculpt clay, paint pottery, or compose a poem or melody in someone's honor, do it!

But why give presents only on birthdays and holidays? If you know your boyfriend loves funny postcards, send him one. If you know your girlfriend loves cool pens, make her day.

Should you peel off the price tag before wrapping a gift? Of course, duh! Unless it was absurdly expensive. Kidding! C'mon, off it goes. Let's not be tacky. (But don't spend too much on each other—gifts often outlast romance.)

By the way, whenever *you* are at the receiving end of a gift, say, "Thank you," not "How much was it?" or "I already have one," or "Mind if I return it for something I like?"

Find the fun in giving, not just getting.

Nobody has ever measured, even the poets,
how much a heart can hold.
—Zelda Fitzgerald

Let's say you're contented, radiant, ecstatic. You catch yourself suppressing a smile during lunch, during science, during track. You go to sleep and wake up thinking about You-Know-Who. And in between, you two are side by side or on the phone or trading e-mails.

Problem is, things can't stay at this fever pitch for years on end. George Bernard Shaw pointed out the difficulty of marriage vows: "When two people are under the influence of the most violent, most insane, most elusive, and most transient of passions, they are required to swear that they will remain in that excited, abnormal, and exhausting condition until death do them part."

You *can* become part of a happily-ever-after couple, but you might, eventually, float earthward. You may still love each other—just not so intensely or insanely every single second. Not to the exclusion of everything else, other thoughts and other people, your studies or your job.

Is this still love?

Absolutely! More muted, perhaps, but also more mature and, in many ways, richer and realer.

Love comes in different hues.

Love burns and also glows.

Love is strong as death; jealousy is cruel as the grave.

—tHE BIBLE, SONG OF SOLOMON

J ealousy may be natural, but it's also a drag.

You like that your significant other is warm, upbeat, and funny, and you can't expect all that charisma to be yours and yours alone. You can feel flattered that most of it is directed toward fabulous, deserving you, but you can't expect an effervescent person to put a lid on it.

So don't drive yourself crazy. Just as you—happily paired-off you—still notice other attractive earthlings out there (admit it, you do), so your beloved has not gone suddenly blind.

Looking is legal. Try to trust each other, not stifle each other.

On the other hand, if your main squeeze and your best friend have been sharing lingering smiles, and their inside jokes are gnarling *your* insides, you are allowed to speak up to either or both of them. Jealous feelings can be an appropriate warning sign, and sometimes with a few words, you can nip trouble in the bud.

Other times it's not so easy. If you learn that your beloved has something else going on the side, it can be difficult to turn things around. And you may not want to. Who needs a disloyal beloved?

Is your love life causing you more pain than fun? You may be better off on your own. Although you don't want to be overly suspicious, you also don't want to be the last to know. And when the writing is on the wall, it's best to read it.

Are you jealous because you are insecure?
Or because you two are in trouble?

One of my problems is that I internalize everything.
I can't express anger; I grow a tumor instead.

Mad at your loved one? Say so rather than seethe in silence or build a permanent grudge. But say what you mean without being mean.

Instead of screaming, "You're a liar! You stood me up!" Say, "You said you'd be there. What happened?"

Instead of shouting, "I can't believe you asked Chris to dance!" Say, "It's because I care about you that I was upset when you asked Chris to dance."

It's better to fight than to pretend everything is fine when it isn't. But don't just accuse or shout or cry. Talk and listen. Be ready to make up and move on.

To avoid or end a quarrel, try a kiss. Or say, "I don't want to fight, do you?" Or, "I need a hug. C'm'ere." Or, "Let's talk about this later"—and then do.

And if it's *you* who owe an apology, apologize. You'll both feel better if you do.

P.S. If an apology is needed but is absolutely, positively beyond you, can you at least sign and send a card with a baby polar bear on the outside and mushy words on the inside?

Speak your mind—but choose your words well.

I scorn you not. It seems you scorn me.

—William Shakespeare

Love can be confusing, but why set out to confuse someone you care about?

When you're upset, do you pass your girlfriend or boyfriend in the hallway as though you haven't been introduced? When you're hurt, do you start flirting with his or her best friend hoping to ignite jealousy? "Lord, what fools these mortals be!" Shakespeare wrote, and you can picture him shaking his head at us all.

I love games—Scrabble, Poker, Hearts, Boggle.* But when it comes to love, playing games is a no-no. Relationships are tricky enough without leaving them to guesswork.

Do you act like you don't care when you do? If so, you may be playing so hard-to-get that you'll never get got. Are you such an out-there flirt that no one can read your heart? If so, you may be leading people on or getting labeled a "player" or a "tease."

Rather than mask your feelings and hope someone figures them out, try being upfront and honest with the person you're involved with. Even if you get shot down—or have to gently let someone else down—it saves time and heartache when people know where they stand, whether on firm ground or quicksand.

* Especially Boggle. I'm killer at Boggle.

Don't play games with other people's hearts.

Once a woman has forgiven her man,
she must not reheat his sins for breakfast.
—marlene Dietrich

If you catch your girlfriend stealing a twenty from your wallet or if your boyfriend admits that for a year now, he's been fooling around with someone else, I don't think you should say, "I forgive you." I think you should say, "You are *so* history."

But what if the crime is less blatant? Just say your sweetie and a cute classmate got together to study and you confess that this bothered you and he/she swears not to schedule any more study sessions. Or just say your honey forgot your birthday but, once prompted, springs for a romantic evening. Should you keep stewing and harping? No. Stewing and harping aren't fun and do not bring out the best in you. Instead, let go of your anger and let your loved one out of the doghouse.

Stay on your guard so you don't get hurt that way again. But if you're going to forgive, forgive fully, not halfway.

"The weak can never forgive," said Mohandas Gandhi. "Forgiveness is the attribute of the strong."

Hold on to the person; let go of the grudge.

But looking into his eyes, she was frightened, realizing that there was not that barrier of modesty she had always felt between herself and other men. She did not know how it was that within five minutes she had come to feel herself terribly near to this man.

—LEO TOLSTOY

Tolstoy again. This time, the subject is chemistry.

Sometimes you and someone else are attracted to each other so quickly and strongly that you can hardly take your eyes off each other. Is this love at first sight? No—though it can develop into love.

But just because you two feel like magnets does not mean the attraction is going to be good for you. Often the other magnet is off-limits (a coach, teacher, ex's sibling, friend's main squeeze, or a way-older married person). Or you may be looking for love whereas the other person is looking for company or a conquest.

So get to know that good-looking stranger before losing your heart. Even then, hold on to your head! If warning bells go off inside you, listen to them.

After all, hot isn't everything. You have to love with your brain, too.

Do you have an impossible crush on a celebrity or someone two continents away? Is this crush fun, or is it making you miserable?

Do your parents dislike the person you like? Ask why and hear them out. Maybe they would disapprove of anyone you brought home. Or maybe they don't like that the person smokes or drinks or cuts class. Can you see their point?

Oscar Wilde said, "The only way to get rid of a temptation is to yield to it." But Wilde was being witty. In real life, sometimes you *have* to talk yourself out of a crush. Even when it's difficult. Really, really difficult.

Cupid can be stupid, but you don't have to be.

I am going to put off reading Lolita for six years, till she's 18.
—Groucho Marx

Your boyfriend or girlfriend is a year (or two) older or younger than you? This may be okay.

But if he or she is much older, this can be a recipe for disaster.

Why be unduly intimidated or impressed by people simply because they happen to be born dozens of months (or many years) before you? Just because someone older has noticed that you have hit puberty and are fabulously attractive does not mean you're supposed to do anything about it. Imagine yourself at eighteen or twenty-eight or thirty-eight. Will you be going after fourteen-year-olds? Why or why not? Though I am sure you are wonderful right now, for a predatory older person, you might be the chance at an easy hook-up instead of the challenge of a relationship.

Most adults are trustworthy. But if an adult in your life ever plunks an arm around you or hits on you, beware. A situation that starts out flattering can become frightening or abusive. Walk away, call for help, or say something like, "That makes me uncomfortable." If an older person asks you out, decline directly, or if it's easier, say, "I'm not allowed to go out at night"(even if you have lots of freedom). If you ever feel scared or threatened, speak to an adult you trust!

Someday rent *The Graduate* or *Smooth Talk*. For now, seek out people around your age. You have the rest of your life to be older.

Protect yourself.

*We didn't realize that we were actually
breaking up as it was happening.*
—Paul McCartney

Some couples part ways almost painlessly. Hugh Grant said of his split with Elizabeth Hurley: "It was as near-perfect a mutual dumping as you can get. It was absolutely 50-50."

But what if one person wants out and the other doesn't? You can try to speak your mind, your heart. You might even get back together—though often just to break up again.

Happy endings are never guaranteed. Where there's pleasure, there can be pain. (In Disney's *The Little Mermaid,* Ariel marries Eric; in the original Hans Christian Andersen story, she hurls herself into the ocean and turns into sea foam! And what about poor Romeo and Juliet?)

Fact is, most middle school and high school couples are not headed toward marriage—which is probably just as well. Everyone is still changing, and you have to find yourself before finding someone else.

Sometimes love just runs its course, or two people who seemed well-suited at fifteen have less in common at seventeen. Other times, people forget to keep appreciating each other.

"A bell is tolling, fading, fading. Just like love. Only poetry lasts," wrote poet Ho Xuan Huong.

If you two usually hang online, but lately you've been checking hour after hour, day after day, and there's never an e-hello, well, as playwright Tennessee Williams wrote, "There is a time for departure even when there's no certain place to go."

When asked if the Beatles might reunite, Paul answered, "You cannot reheat a soufflé."

Breakups hurt. Breakups happen.

It is no time to swap horses when you are crossing the stream.
−aвraнam lincoln

You know Gershwin's song, "Let's Call the Whole Thing Off"? The one about potatoes and po-tah-toes? "You say eether and I say eyether, you say neether and I say nyther . . ."

Don't pull the plug on a relationship for a dumb reason, but don't let one limp along for old time's sake either. (Eyther?)

While getting dumped is awful, so is being the one to end the relationship. Why? Because if you ever really cared about someone, and your heart isn't full of rocks, then you hate to hurt that person.

Timing matters. Don't announce that you two are history right before history finals or while exchanging corsages on prom night.

Do the deed alone, not in the lunchroom or on the school bus or before an audience. Don't just avoid each other either, as George Costanza did on *Seinfeld*. ("If she can't find me," he reasoned, "she can't break up with me.")

Finally, don't break up online or through a friend. Do it in person if possible. Strive to be honest, not hurtful. Don't say, "You're full of yourself and I'm already with someone better." Try, for instance, "I like you but I don't think things are working between us," or "I'm really sorry, but my feelings have changed," or "I care about you but I think we're too young to get serious." (Then be decent enough *not* to be caught holding hands with someone else the next day.) And don't trash the person or make mutual friends pick sides. Try to stay on okay terms with everyone, including your ex. It's hard, but it's doable. (I know because I've done it.)

Close the door; don't slam it.

Where you used to be, there is a hole in the world,
which I find myself constantly walking around in the daytime,
and falling in at night. I miss you like hell.
—edna St. Vincent Millay

Whether you're the one leaving or the one being left, it's undeniably sad when the *ove* of *love* becomes the *ove* of *over*.

But just as the relationship didn't last forever, the misery won't either. And while pain stinks, it isn't permanent. So plod along, and if you feel like crying, cry. (Guys, this means you, too.)

But then . . . change the channel! Go for a swim. Meet friends for pizza. Cook something. Build something. Play music. Volunteer. Keep a journal. Pet your cat. Plan a getaway weekend. Draw. Rent a movie. Read a book. (Oops. I guess you *are* reading a book!)

When love makes an exit, let a flurry of activities sweep in to take its space. Staying busy and involved, even when your smashed-up heart isn't in it, is the surest way to start feeling good again. That and having someone to talk to—a best friend, parent, cousin, confidant, or counselor. (But no, not your ex's sexy twin.)

Pakistani poet Faiz Ahmed Faiz wrote: "Patience, my heart: Night's length will pass."

Can you take three giant steps back? Can you see all the good things that are still in your life? Can you use your hurt to become more compassionate or to create art?

"Do you believe in life after love?" Cher asked. I do. And as k.d. lang pointed out, "There's nothing like a good heartbreak to get a good song."

From pain, a painting?

Yes, I've been hurt. I've suffered. But that's not what makes me me. What makes me me is getting through all that stuff, pushing it aside, moving forward.

—Jennifer Love Hewitt

"If you don't have the wound of a broken heart, how do you know you're alive?" asks Man in an Edward Albee play. Most of us have hearts with nicks, dents, and scars. Hearts aren't made of Teflon. But they are strong and resilient. And broken ones mend.

Have you been dismissed or voted off the island? Your ex may have done you a favor because now you're available to meet a better match. Someone too smart to let you go.

"Being jilted is one of life's most painful experiences," Frank Sinatra said. "It's happened to all of us and never gets any easier. I understand, however, that playing one of my albums can help." It also helps to remind yourself of the things about your ex that drove you crazy—the ones you kept trying to ignore. And it helps to hang out with your friends—the ones you didn't dump the second you started going out.

Soon (but please, not tomorrow or even the day after), you will fall in love again. Or maybe this time you will *step* in.

For now, you aren't half a couple; you're a whole person.

Sunrise follows sunset, and more heart-to-hearts are in your future. As Milton Kellum wrote: "Got along without ya before I met ya, gonna get along without ya now."

Your hurt is already healing.

Your life is opening up, not closing.

And love *is* worth it.

This was just one chapter. There are more chapters ahead.

Hearts have lots of chambers.

SCHOOL

The way out of the cotton patch is through the schoolhouse door.
—MARY ELIZABETH DAVIDSON LITTLE

I f the name above doesn't ring a bell, it's because she was my great-grandmother—a poor Texan farmer with sky-high standards. Her three sons all went on to become doctors; two got MDs and one got a Ph.D.

Even if you hate school, try to struggle through it. Enlist friends or tutors or attend summer school, but don't quit before getting your high school diploma. And after that, keep going.

Having a degree almost always translates into more interests, more confidence, and more money.

Malcolm X said, "Without education, you're not going anywhere in this world."

If you don't graduate when you're young,
you'll regret it when you're old.

He missed Hogwarts so much it was like having
a constant stomachache.
—J. K. Rowling

Everyone loves snow days, spring break, three-day weekends, and summer vacation. But school isn't all bad, and some kids, like Harry Potter, love being there.

School is your chance to see friends five days a week. To have lunch with people you care about. To play sports and do art and join an after-school program.

School is where you can discover interests, develop skills, unlock strengths. You may not like every subject every day, but there must be at least one you do enjoy. And while conjugating foreign verbs or memorizing dates may not be anybody's idea of a good time, being able to speak another language or hold your own in a discussion about Pearl Harbor feels good. There are payoffs to studying hard.

In the olden days, not everyone even had the right to an education.

Today, education is still a privilege. The more you learn, the more you'll understand, the more comfortable you'll be with adults, the more you'll get all the jokes on *Saturday Night Live*, and the readier you'll be to forge your future.

It's your turn to learn.

Teach thy tongue to say, "I do not know."
—maimonides

You're not supposed to get everything the first time. If people expected you to be an expert, you'd be teaching courses instead of taking them. So when you don't understand a lab result, or Civil War battle, or the ablative in Latin, or when to say *savoir* instead of *connaître*, chances are, others are also confused.

Ask questions. Get help on small problems before they become big problems.

You're not a moron if you don't know the word oxymoron,[*] but it's a shame if you're unwilling to say, "Could you explain that again, please?"

Be eager to fill the holes in your knowledge.

As William Shakespeare put it, "The fool doth think he is wise, but the wise man knows himself to be a fool."

Halle Berry said, "I'm always the first one to say I don't know what the hell I'm doing. It doesn't make me feel inferior to say that. I think that's why people are open to mentoring me. I'm like a sponge. Show me, show me."

As for playing dumb on purpose, don't do it—unless you want to play with dummies!

---

[*] Psst, *cold fire* is an oxymoron—a figure of speech that appears, at first, to be a contradiction. Like *small crowd*. Or *jumbo shrimp*. Or *silent scream*. Or, some might argue, *pretty ugly, definite maybe, same difference,* and *bigger half*.

When you need help, yelp!

Switching classes and having seven teachers is a lot more
interesting than being in one classroom all the time.
—HaLeY JOeL OSMenT

I f you don't like your current teacher or principal or classroom, keep the faith. The grade you're in lasts just one year.

Besides, just as middle school can be more interesting than grade school, high school can be more interesting than middle school, and college can be the best of all. Why? Because instead of having one teacher, you have many. You get to choose more of your own courses and meet tons of new people. And many of the students in your classes will be learning because they want to be there, not because they have to be there.

In college, you can immerse yourself in whatever you want to study. You want to read novels? Become an English major! You have a passion for architecture? Film? Computers? Fruit flies? Go for it! You want to study something totally different? Flip through the course book—I took classes in surrealism, folklore, and Samuel Beckett.

What if you *never* want to tackle a particular subject again? You may not have to. If you ace an Advanced Placement exam, you may be able to place out of a science, language, or other college requirement.

While many people don't go to college, even more do. Afterward, some go to med school, law school, or grad school where they can study their chosen field to the exclusion of all else.

School gets more interesting as you go along.

A teacher affects eternity;

he can never tell where his influence stops.

—Henry Adams

Teaching is a noble profession.

Teachers aren't in it for the money. They're in it for you. They love their subject and want to pass on the passion. "To encourage excellence is to go beyond the encouraged mediocrity of our society," said Audre Lorde.

Who's your hardest teacher? I used to complain about demanding teachers, but now I realize I learned a lot in their classes. Would you really prefer a teacher who dumbed-down everything? (In "The History Teacher," poet laureate Billy Collins wrote, "Trying to protect his students' innocence, he told them the Ice Age was really just the Chilly Age, a period of a million years when everyone had to wear sweaters.")

Your teachers will not all be favorites. Some may be sexist or rigid or boring—just as some of your future bosses may be. But the best ones? You'll remember them forever. You may even end up consulting with them after class about homework or subjects off their subject. Some teachers become friends.

Do you ever pass favorite former teachers in the hall? Don't walk by as though they don't look familiar. Give a nod of recognition. It's the decent thing to do.

Savvy, too. After all, can you really request a letter of recommendation for school or a job if you stopped being nice the moment you stopped being graded?

Appreciate your good teachers.

Organized education gives us information,
but there are things we have to learn ourselves.
—LaurYn HILL

"If you don't learn history," said architect Maya Lin, "how can you learn?" Piet Hein answered the question "Who Is Learned?" with this poem:

One who, consuming midnight oil
in studies diligent and slow,
teaches himself, with painful toil,
the things that other people know.

It is important to learn history and the discoveries of the past. But it is also important to live—and learn—in the present.

Book smarts count. So do street smarts and the ability to laugh and get along and open up and manage your heart.

When he was president of Yale, Kingman Brewster welcomed my freshman class, saying, "This is primarily a place for learning, but not all learning is in books or laboratories or classrooms." Exactly.

Study breaks can be plenty educational. You can learn a lot from teachers—and from other students.

Learn in class and out.

Little strokes fell great oaks.

—Ben Franklin

Y our plate is full? Don't get overwhelmed—get started!
Take that first step. Brainstorm. Scribble down notes and ideas, large and small, good and less good. Try to visualize the project completed. Figure out which chapter or chunk to tackle first—the first one or hardest one or most appealing one.

Sometimes a children's book can help you find your way into an assignment. Why? Because children's books can tell the story of Helen Keller or Hank Aaron or Hiroshima in forty-eight pages or fewer. With pictures, no less.

Speaking of children's books, author Paula Danziger said, "My favorite book as a kid was *The Little Engine That Could*. I still go, 'I think I can, I think I can,' when I'm feeling insecure."

You can also talk to a parent or friend about ways to break a project into bite-size bits. Talking to yourself helps, too—but don't try this in the lunchroom.

Preparing for an exam? Make yourself double-sided Q and A flash cards if you're learning dates in history. Go over problems you got wrong if you're studying math. Translate lists of words back and forth for your language test.

Turn off the TV, glue your butt to the chair, and make real progress. If your room is too distracting, work elsewhere. Once you get going, you may actually get into it. As the saying goes, "Yard by yard, it's very hard. But inch by inch, it's a cinch."

Step by step.

You have to begin drawing to know
what you want to draw.
—Pablo Picasso

E verybody procrastinates. It's easier to say, "Tomorrow is another day,"
as Margaret Mitchell's Scarlett O'Hara famously did, than to make
headway on homework. And it's easier to say, "I don't know what to write
about," than to sit down and work it out.

Problem is, if you don't get started, you'll never finish.

The best reason for blasting through homework sooner versus later
is that then you can be carefree and spontaneous. If you finish your
homework on Saturday, and someone calls on Sunday with an extra
ticket to a concert or game, you can say yes, guilt-free. Or *you* can be
the one to plan to meet a friend and see a movie.

Still having trouble buckling down? Maybe you need a plan. "A
schedule defends from chaos and whim," wrote Annie Dillard. Or maybe
you need an incentive. Perhaps your reward for knocking off an assignment is making a call, going online, or watching MTV or a video. Me,
when I finish this page, I get a Ghirardelli Dark Chocolate Square.

Hey, whatever works.

Now's the time.

A good garden may have some weeds.

—thomas fuller

N ow that I've pointed out the virtues of Now, let me add that some people are so hard on themselves that what *they* need is not more pressure or organizational strategies, but to kick back and cut themselves some slack.

Are you such a perfectionist that you stay up past midnight dotting *i*s and crossing *t*s when your homework was in good shape before the clock struck ten? Do you expect all *A*s all the time? Do you study for hours for every little quiz? Do you say things like, "If I don't get into Princeton or Stanford, I'll just die?"

Ease up! Chill out! You're still a minor—you don't have to pay the rent or worry about insurance or shoulder the worries of the world.

Grades aren't everything.

There's no such thing as perfect, and you don't have to get it all done right now.

Do your best, sure. But don't overdo it.

Shooting for perfect is okay, but so is shooting pool and shooting hoops.

Sometimes you have to take it easy—
even if that's not easy for you.

The only thing that makes me truly happy is mathematics.

—peter Høeg

D o you revel in the precision of numbers, the equation that works, QED? Do you love how, unlike life, math *is* black and white, right and wrong?

If you are able to understand hypotenuses and logarithms and cosines, you probably enjoy the on-top-of-it feeling that comes with being able to master a subject others find daunting.

If, however, you're among the daunted, you're not alone. When I took math and got it, it felt great. Sometimes I couldn't figure out how I figured it out, I was just glad it worked.

But sometimes I did *not* get it, and that felt *not* great. Thank heavens for my friend David Sherwood who untangled impossible word problems. (Wait. Why am I thanking heavens? I should thank Dave himself!) Dave, wherever you are, thanks!

Not everyone loves math. Or shines in math. But we all need basic math to balance checkbooks, collect payments, leave tips, or calculate how many hot dogs to buy for a barbecue. Or even to make music. Alicia Keys says she has used math in her work because, "Math is very musical, and music is very mathematical."

So stick it out and get help if necessary, because if you fall behind in math, it does get harder and harder to catch up.

Math matters.

The most beautiful thing we can experience is the mysterious.
It is the source of all true art and science.
—albert einstein

I s science the subject that gets you juiced? Maybe you love to understand animals, study stars, decode periodic tables, run experiments, and figure out how hearts beat, trees grow, fish swim, and clocks tick.

Maybe you love knowing that there's always more to know. More to examine and reexamine.

"Doubt is the beginning of knowledge," said Aristotle.

"Science is believing in the ignorance of scientists," said physicist Richard Feynman.

"Research is formalized curiosity. It is poking and prying with a purpose," said Zora Neale Hurston.

Think about which subjects interest you and make you want to keep poking, keep learning.

Make a discovery.

Everybody who reads has a first book—maybe not the first book you read, but the first book that shows you what literature can be. And you read other books, you kiss other people, but especially for those who are romantically inclined, that first book stays with you.

—michael cunningham

Do you have a first book—besides *Hop on Pop*? Maybe *Harry Potter* or *Charlotte's Web*? *The Phantom Tollbooth* or *Old Yeller* or *The Giver*? *A Tree Grows in Brooklyn*; *A Separate Peace*; *The Catcher in the Rye*? *The Lord of the Rings*—or *Lord of the Flies*?

"A novel, after a single reading, sticks to your ribs for a lifetime," wrote Graydon Carter. "The great ones do, anyway." He's right. You can read a novel once and remember it forever. And many novels (like *The Great Gatsby*) are so good, they are worth rereading.

"A great book should leave you with many experiences and slightly exhausted at the end. You should lead several lives while reading it," said writer William Styron.

You may think you have too much assigned reading to allow for any pleasure reading. But according to Mark Twain, "The man who does not read good books has no advantage over the man who can't read them." And it's a shame to read only what's required. Reading can be a joy, an escape, a way to unwind. Books keep you company when you're alone or stuck on a line or when you're waiting for a friend. Readers are never bored. And isn't it nice to know that Victor Hugo and Edith Wharton and Aesop are ready to tell you a story whenever you'd like to hear one?

"The grandeur of learning to read, of knowing words," said basketball great Walt "Clyde" Frasier, "can change your life, like it changed my life."

Put books by your bed.

You never know when a lovely idea is going to flit suddenly into your mind, but by golly, when it does come along, you grab it with both hands and hang on tight. The trick is to write it down at once, otherwise you'll forget.

—roald Dahl

Good thing Roald Dahl took his ideas seriously. When he got inspired, he didn't say, "What a stupid idea—how could I even think it?" or "What a great idea—I'm sure I'll remember it." No. The idea presented itself, Dahl held on tight, and the world is a better place because of *Matilda, The BFG,* and *Charlie and the Chocolate Factory* (which may have been my "first book").

When you get a good idea, capture it. On a napkin if necessary. With a crayon if necessary. But don't just figure it will reappear when you need it. Ideas are shy and have pathetically fragile egos. They need to be handled with care. If you don't appreciate them right away, they don't always give you a second chance.

Ideas also have terrible timing. They often come not when you're at your desk, but when you're running or in the shower. When this happens, write them down as soon as you can—even if you are dripping water or dripping sweat. You can always discard an idea in the future, but you cannot always retrieve an idea from the past.

British philosopher Alfred North Whitehead said, "Ideas won't keep: something must be done about them." Next time you have an idea, jot it down. Or set it in motion!

Take care of your ideas.

By the time I finish my first draft, I've written between
the lines and around the edges and on the back
of the paper. It's a mess.

—BEVERLY CLEARY

After you have filled a page and before you hand it in, there's a step most people skip: proofreading.

I write fairly quickly. Then I tinker and tweak and cross out and add on and revise and edit, all of which takes forever. But I cannot, in one sitting, do a good job of writing and rewriting. Why? Because when I'm writing, I'm trying to be creative, inspired, uncensored. When I'm rewriting, I'm trying to be critical, nitpicky, fault-finding.

If you're thinking, *I don't have to proofread because I have spell check*, think again. Spell check won't save you. It May knot eve in fined olive yore miss steaks. And it definitely won't help if you don't know *it's* versus *its*; *too, two, to*; and *there, they're, their*. (There, there, there, not to worry. As a public service, I'm about to discuss all that and more on the very next pages.)

"All I know about grammar is its power," wrote Joan Didion.

Punctuation counts, too. "Woman, without her man, is nothing" has a different meaning from "Woman: Without her, man is nothing." Even spaces matter: "We went to get her" does not equal "We went together."

Of course, rereading your draft is not just about correcting mistakes. It's about making sure you are saying what you set out to say. Take the time to rework your work, scribble over it, make it better.

Neatness counts only at the end.

Don't just write; rewrite.

English? Who needs that? I'm never going to England.

—Homer Simpson

It's/its	*It's* not that hard. *It's* is the contraction of *it* and *is*. *Its* (even though it lacks an apostrophe) is possessive. Example: *It's* true! You shouldn't judge a book by *its* cover.
To/too/two	*Too* many students (not just one or *two*) don't take the time *to* use the right *to* or *too* or *two*. I hope you do. (A poem!)
There/they're/their	Were you *there* when your teacher explained that *they're* is a contraction and *their* is possessive? *There* are lots of quotes in this book. *They're* from famous folks. Do you like *their* words of wisdom?
A lot	"Alot"? 'Fraid not. *A lot* is *a lot* of words.
Less/fewer	Use *less* when it's a general quantity; use *fewer* when you can count the amount. *Less* money; *fewer* dollars. *Less* water; *fewer* puddles. Got it? Great—you will make *fewer* mistakes.
Your/you're	*You're* is a contraction. *Your* is possessive. Example: *You're* lucky *your* vacation is next week. Uh-oh. Confession time. In high school my wonderful boyfriend wrote me, "Your wonderful." My heart skipped a beat . . . but I did notice the mistake.

Whether you're writing an e-mail, love letter, class paper, or office memo, keep mistakes to a minimum. People do notice. Even nice, non-judgmental people like me.

Why not get it right?

Is sloppiness in speech caused by ignorance or apathy?
I don't know and I don't care.
—WILLIAM Safire

J ust when you thought you were safe, another grammar page! Learn this now, and you'll own it forever.

Matt and I   "Matt and me" is wrong as the subject of a sentence. "*Matt and I* are friends" is correct.

Between you and me   Just *between you and me*, "Between you and I" is *always* wrong—even when someone says it on TV. (And even if a teacher does!)

Preposition me!   Take it *from me*, the correct wording is, "She went to the party with Emily and me." Remove the person's name and you'll realize that you would never say, "*with I*" or "*to I*" or "*from I*" or "*by I.*" So don't say, "He talked to Emily and I." After a preposition, it's *me*. Are you *with me me me*? Good!

As I said   "*As I said*" is correct. "*Like I said*" is common but incorrect.

My dad liked to tell this story: Winston Churchill wrote a speech and ended a sentence with (gasp!) a preposition. An assistant "corrected" it. Churchill, perhaps to show that some rules should be bent, wrote in the margin: "This is an impertinence up with which I will not put."

Don't just be smart. Sound smart.

Never use a long word when a short one will do.

—george orwell

Back to Editing 101. Before handing in your paper, delete a few of the SAT words and highfalutin ones like *thus* or *heretofore*. As Orwell also advised: "If it is possible to cut a word out, always cut it out."

In short, be concise. Why say, "keep the lines of communication open" when you can say "talk"? Why use psychobabble when you can be clear? Unless someone is extraordinarily eloquent, when he or she uses big words—excuse me, employs polysyllabic vocabulary—it obscures meaning and makes the person sound more insecure than brainy.

Think of your first draft as a sopping wet sponge and wring the extra words out of it.

One way to tighten your final draft is to read it aloud. Maybe to your mom. Maybe to your mirror. But read it with an ear for repetitive or awkward words or phrases. Your ears may pick up what your eyes missed.

Finally, if someone is willing to look over your work—your father, sister, brilliant friend—and that "editor" can make constructive suggestions without deflating you, do not be defensive. Be grateful, very grateful. (I am! Just check out my Acknowledgments page!)

Make your point.

I want to write—I want to write—I want to write and
I never will. I know it and I am so unhappy and it seems
as though nothing else mattered.
—anne morrow Lindbergh

Despite the worries of her youth, Anne Morrow Lindbergh did write. She wrote over two dozen books of prose and poetry, and they sold in the millions.

Sometimes what you need is patience.

Other times you need permission.

Nobel Prize–winning author Gabriel García Márquez wrote, "One night a friend lent me a book of short stories by Franz Kafka . . . I began reading *The Metamorphosis*. The first line almost knocked me off the bed. . . . 'As Gregor Samsa awoke that morning from uneasy dreams, he found himself transformed in his bed into a gigantic insect . . .' I didn't know anyone was allowed to write things like that. . . . So I immediately started writing stories."

In my book, writing counts, and since this *is* my book, allow me to quote one more author. Novelist Allegra Goodman said she's not intimidated by the Great Writers—Shakespeare, Cervantes, Dante, Zola—and you shouldn't be either. "Oh, they still cast their shadow, but I'm alive, and they are irrefutably dead. Their language is exquisite, their stories divine, but what have these writers done lately? Not a damn thing. Think about it. The idea should give you hope. . . . Your masterpiece could be just around the corner."

Writer's block, schmiter's block. Writing can be liberating and fun, so sharpen your pencil and let loose!

Give yourself permission.

I want to go on living even after my death! And therefore I am grateful to God for giving me this gift, this possibility of developing myself and of writing, of expressing all that is in me.

—anne frank

nne Frank grew up in a time of horror and inhumanity. She was Jewish, and because Hitler and the Nazis were hunting down Jews, she and her family had to live in hiding for over two years during World War II. On August 4, 1944, they were caught and sent to concentration camps, and the next spring, Anne died of typhus at age fifteen. Her life ended tragically, and she was just one of millions of victims. But because of her gift, Anne Frank *has* gone on living after death. She has become the most famous girl author in the world. And thanks to her gift the way she used her talent and kept her diary—readers young and old have learned about the Holocaust.

What is your gift? How might you affect the world? How can you develop it further in school?

Can you write, sketch, play the guitar, relate to people? Can you sing, dance, drum? If you have a talent, why be shy or lazy about it? Use it. Be generous with it. "God gives everybody gifts. You just have to realize what *yours* is and work on that," said Beyoncé Knowles of Destiny's Child.

In many cases, your talent will give others pleasure and enrich your life. In a few cases, it will let you go on living forever.

"The beauty of the body perishes, but a work of art does not," said Leonardo da Vinci. He's right. Mona Lisa herself has been dead as a doornail for centuries, but if you go to the Louvre, she will smile serenely at you and follow you with her eyes. And Leonardo will be behind her, smiling, too, invisible and immortal.

Open your gift and share it.

I just knew that was the world I belonged to.

It was so clear to me.

—JULIEttE BINOCHE

Some lucky people have always known what they wanted to do. "I was more or less born with a pen in my hand," said writer Harold Pinter.

Some don't find their path until they are in their twenties or much older.

And many, such as actress Juliette Binoche, figure out where they belong during school.

Maybe theater is your world. You audition and get a part or you work backstage rigging props or operating lights, and you realize: *This is it; this makes me happy.*

Or maybe it's in shop or in the chorus or the darkroom or at a political meeting that you feel most alive.

Though you're busy with required classes, keep sampling the other activities—other worlds—that your school has to offer.

If your school has an art department, work with watercolors or oils or clay or film. In real life, it's hard for grown-ups to fill a canvas or throw a pot or make a movie out of the blue. But in school, dabbling is encouraged.

So dabble! Invite the arts into your life. For your sake and—depending on your luck, talent, and discipline—for everyone else's.

If you have a passion, run with it. Because while it's good to be a well-rounded well-balanced person, it's cool to be a pointy person, too. Or a lopsided one who kicks butt at one particular thing. (Many colleges look for well-angled applicants, not just well-rounded ones.)

Pursue your passions. Find your world.

I didn't like my life very much—didn't like school, didn't like anything—so it was a choice between getting a machine gun or an instrument. Luckily, I found an instrument.

—artie SHaW

Is music your talent?

Despite budget cuts, many schools provide the chance to sing in choruses or glee clubs or musicals or to play in bands or jazz ensembles or orchestras. Some teach music appreciation.

Outside school, you can try to teach yourself an instrument or take private music lessons or join a church choir or form a group with friends.

Louis Armstrong borrowed money and bought his first cornet at a pawn shop. Look where it took him!

Bob Dylan said, "I realized I could do it effortlessly—that I could sing night after night after night and never get tired."

Even if you're not going pro, your life will be richer if you set it to music.

Try to *listen* to music, not just hear it. Tune your radio to more than just one station. Go to more than one kind of concert. Listen to new and old stuff.

Music is powerful. Some of your CDs can probably lift you out of the darkest of moods. Figure out which ones and treasure them.

"Music," wrote Henry Wadsworth Longfellow, "is the universal language of mankind."

In school and out, add music to your life.

Let there be music.

In order to excel, you must be completely dedicated to
your chosen sport.

—WILLIE MAYS

"B ecause of baseball, I smelled the rose of life," said "Cool Papa" Bell, who played on the Negro League in the 1920s, 1930s, and 1940s. "It allowed me to become a member of a brotherhood of friendship that will last forever."

Can you be part of a club or team—part of a family of friends with a common passion and a healthy sense of competition and cooperation? Is your sport baseball, soccer, football, basketball, volleyball, lacrosse, swimming, tennis, skating, track, gymnastics, fencing, cheerleading, or water polo? Bowling? Biking? Something else?

Sports aren't just good for your body. They're good for your soul, your social life, your self-esteem, and for appreciating your body for what it does, not just how it looks.

Some people play to belong, others play to have fun, or to exercise, or to win. If you play to win, consider these words of World Golf Hall of Famer Nancy Lopez: "Successful competitors want to win. Head cases want to win at all costs."

Join a team.

I was thrown out of NYU my freshman year for cheating on my metaphysics final. I looked within the soul of the boy sitting next to me.

—WOODY ALLEN

If you cheat, you're shortchanging yourself. Why? Because if you don't learn the material for the test, you won't know the material at all. Not only will you never be a lifeline on *Who Wants to Be a Millionaire?*, but you'll feel less confident. If you never learn how to spell, you'll feel unsure when you pen a letter. If you can't figure out percentages, you'll worry every time you have to tip a waiter or cabbie. If you don't know *ser* from *estar*, you won't master Spanish.

As Nick Lachey of 98 Degrees said, "Don't cheat, because it's just not worth it. You'd lose so much more than you'd gain." When you work hard, you earn a self-respect worth more than grades.

What about plagiarizing? This book is filled with other people's wisdom. But I quote people—I don't pretend I wrote their words.

In the age of the Internet, it's easy to cut and paste and plagiarize . . . and easy to get caught. Your teachers have computers, too, so if your words ring familiar, or if you hand in a terrific term paper when you haven't done squat all semester, teachers can find you out. You get busted, your parents get called, and the principal has to decide whether to suspend or expel you.

Don't steal someone else's work. Do your own. Then credit your sources with fancy footnotes and an impressive bibliography. (Bonus: Teachers eat up fancy footnotes and impressive bibliographies.)

Cheating cheats you.

Every school has 'em. See, you start a new school, you get your

desks, some blackboards, and some mean kids.

—Xander Harris in *Buffy the Vampire Slayer*

Most schools have a few mean kids. Maybe they are unhappy. Maybe some adult is mean to them and they are out for revenge. Whatever the reason, mean kids are like bees, and if you don't bother them, they usually won't bother you. So try to stay out of their way.

But what if *you* are getting harassed?

Teasing happens (good-natured and otherwise), but harassment is when someone is continually making pointed, unwelcome, offensive (and sometimes sexist) comments that get in the way of your work. If someone, peer or adult, keeps touching you inappropriately or saying, "Cute butt," every time you sit at your desk, and you've said, "Cut it out," but the person won't, that may constitute harassment.

Keep a record of what is said and when. That way you can back up a complaint. Depending on the situation, you can then either tell the person, "One more comment and I'll report you," or go ahead and report it to your teacher, adviser, principal, school counselor, or parent and ask what he or she will do to help.

Try to put space between yourself and the mean kids.

Violence is almost like a strong pill. It may work in one way,
but the side effects may be equally strong.

—the Dalai Lama

Statistically, schools are wonderfully safe, so don't worry. But unless you're way overprotected and have been bobbing along in your own little world, you are probably aware that every so often, a school shooting makes headline news.

You know how a person should never joke about bombs or knives when he is about to board an airplane because it's the security officer's job to boot him off the flight? Nowadays, if you say, "I'm going to kill her," or "I wish he were dead!" and the principal overhears you, you could be toast. Hauled off, interrogated, suspended, or expelled. Words are powerful. Do not use them loosely.

What if *you* overhear someone mutter, "I could kill that teacher"? If it's your sweet-natured sister letting off steam at home, roll with it. But if it's someone who gives you the creeps or who owns guns and is cruel to animals, why let the comment slide? Pass the information to an adult you trust and ask to remain anonymous. That's not tattling. That's being responsible.

"I grew up way too fast today," said Tabitha Vess, who was seventeen and at Santana High School during the shoot-out there on March 5, 2001. "I want to be a kid again."

Do what you can to stop violence.

It bothers me that there is an image of me being

so . . . nauseatingly good.

—Sally Field

Just as there are bullies in your school, there are goody-goodies, too. If you are a straight-A student, and you sometimes wish you were more wild and carefree, be proud, not self-conscious, about your grades. Anyone teasing you would probably love to bring home your report card. Don't spend all your time studying, but don't yearn to be someone you're not, either. Spiking your hair or piercing your tongue might shake up your reputation, but would not make the you inside feel different.

Is there more to you than meets the eye? Of course. No one can be described in one word. So keep exploring nonacademic pursuits. Show people that you're not only an A student, you're a multifaceted person. A linguist or saxophonist or horseback rider or skateboarder or card shark or the one to ask if you have a question about bugs or Botticelli, old movies or Olympics, teen celebrities or world news.

Show people your other sides.

I wish it would be compulsory for every high school kid to experience a different culture for two weeks and be forced to eat something other than fast food.

—Susan Sarandon

I spent a month after tenth grade living on a farm in southern France with the Experiment in International Living Program. I vaccinated sheep, gathered snails, and learned French. It was *fantastique* (despite a brief bout of homesickness), so I applied to a program called School Year Abroad and spent all of twelfth grade with a different French family in Brittany. I walked the beaches of D day, visited medieval Mont-Saint-Michel, and still took AP exams and applied to college.

Intrigued? Once you're an adult (and especially if you're a working parent), it is much much harder (trust me!) to grab a year and hop an airplane. But a student can join a foreign family and make faraway friends. And as author Juan Goytisolo said, "To have two languages and cultures is better than one, three better than two."

Some travel programs involve homestays, language classes, or volunteering. Some are pure adventure. All are fun and eye-opening and provide a glimpse of the globe, plus a way for you to see your own world with a new perspective. Check online, quiz your librarian, and start saving money or looking into scholarships.

You say you can't miss the Snow Ball Prom or Senior Prank Day or the chance to be a lifeguard? Okay. But are you *sure* you can miss a semester or summer in another continent and the opportunity to learn another language? "The further you travel, the longer you live," wrote Chinese author Ma Jian.

And home sweet home will be there when you return.

Living abroad is broadening.

I don't care if going to college ruins my career. I'd rather be smart than be a movie star.

—Natalie Portman

Stage and screen actress Natalie Portman is already smart, because it's not either/or and she gets to have it both ways: go to Harvard and be a star of stage and screen.

Want to be a famous actor or musician or athlete? Great! But don't drop out and just hope for the best. Alas, there are thousands of wannabes who never find their way to stardom. Some sing in nightclubs; most wait tables. And many are bitter, especially if they believed that Movie Star (or Rock Star or NFL MVP) was a realistic career option, so they didn't finish their education before going down that path.

For most mortals, finishing school makes more sense than hitting the streets with huge dreams but no degree. It's not that you should turn your back on your talent or on who you are. Get out there and practice your craft, instrument, or sport, and network, too.

But please, have a backup plan. Finish school. After all, college lasts a few years. Education lasts a lifetime.

Aim high—but keep your feet on the ground.

Give me a museum and I'll fill it.

—PABLO PICASSO

D o you think art museums are b-o-r-i-n-g? Not me. I love them.

To enjoy the masterpieces of literature, you need time. Even seeing a movie or play takes hours. But to take in a masterpiece of art, you just need to look at it. You can breathe in the serenity of Vermeer's *Girl With a Pearl Earring* in moments. You can recognize the dignity of Velázquez's *Juan de Pareja* in seconds.

It has always amazed me that you can wander the halls of art museums in an afternoon and enjoy beauty that took great painters and sculptors years—centuries—to create.

I also love that, in a museum, *I'm* in charge. If I like a painting, I keep looking. If I don't, I walk on. I'm never stuck and there are no commercials. I'm also standing as close to colorful canvases as did Francisco de Goya, Vincent van Gogh, Mary Cassatt, or Frida Kahlo. I'm looking *right at* what they touched, what they saw, what they painted.

If you live near an art museum (or history or science museum), you're lucky. And if you haven't visited a museum in a while, give one a try, alone or with a friend or on a date.

No art museums near you? Even leafing through art books can be surprisingly satisfying.

"When you have a really good film or a good book or even a good painting," said Nicole Kidman, "there is always something else to see in it."

"My painting is what I have to give back to the world for what the world gives to me," said Georgia O'Keeffe.

Open your heart to art.

I have always imagined that Paradise will be a kind of library.

−JOrge Borges

I love libraries. The proud shelves of slim picture books and fat encyclopedias. The welcoming tables and inviting desks. The wonder of being surrounded by thinkers, scholars, poets, and storytellers. The smell and heft and calm of so many books, new and worn. The possibility of working uninterrupted for hours. The permission to be antisocial and bookish.

It was in a library that I began writing the first article I ever published (for *Seventeen*) and began reading the longest novel I ever read (*War and Peace*).

Does your school or town have a good library?

Sometimes you go to a library because you know you'll run into friends. Others times you go because you know you need to focus. In a library, you don't have to plead with anyone to turn down the music or take the phone into another room. You don't even have to argue with yourself about whether you should be practicing the flute or outside enjoying the sunshine.

When you go to a library, it's to work. And so you do.

You track down the fact you need with a peace and purposefulness that you cannot truly feel in front of a computer screen. Or you nestle in among the rows of books to read. Or write. Or dream.

"Come and take choice of all my library, and so beguile thy sorrow," said William Shakespeare.

Where can you concentrate? Where can you get into a "work bubble"? At home? At school? In a library? Work where you work best.

Love your library.

School never ends. The classroom is everywhere.

*—*anna quinblen

Mahatma Gandhi said, "Live as if you were to die tomorrow. Learn as if you were to live forever."

Are you living and learning outside the classroom?

Are your eyes and ears open? Are you reading and observing and thinking? Are you getting smarter, wiser, more knowledgable?

That, not grades, is the whole point of school.

School does not end when the bell rings.

FAMILY

Home is where one starts from.

—t. S. eliot

What can you do to promote world peace! Mother Teresa asked
upon receiving the Nobel Peace Prize. "Go home and love your
family."

Before you know it, you will be in college or on your own. Right now,
your family is your home. And chances are, they love you and you love
them—no matter how you all do or don't show it.

While your future is not yet clear, your present and past is with
family.

"Nobody leaps into the air from the air," wrote novelist Richard Russo.
"We all leap into the air from something solid."

Home is a good four-letter word.

Make the best of your nest.

Mr. and Mrs. Dursley, of number four, Privet Drive,

were proud to say they were perfectly normal,

thank you very much.

—J. K. ROWLING

What is perfectly normal and who'd want to be it?

"I think very few people are completely normal, really," wrote Noel Coward, "deep down in their private lives."

As for normal families, is there even such a thing?

Most kids do not have family situations as complicated as Harry Potter's, but millions of kids do not live with both biological birth parents. "Traditional" or "nuclear" families (meaning: Mom and Dad and their kids) make up *fewer* than one fourth of American households. Like Harry, lots of children live with relatives or in stepfamilies or adoptive families. Many split their time between two families. Many live with single mothers or single fathers, or with a mother and her boyfriend, or with a father and his girlfriend, or with parents with gay partners.

Families come in all sizes and flavors—with and without sprinkles and nuts!

Think your family is unusual? Look around.

A normal adolescent isn't a normal adolescent

if he acts normal.

—JUDITH VIORST

Teenagers sometimes act moody and rebellious. It's almost a given. Groucho Marx—a teenager at heart—said, "Whatever it is, I'm against it!"

Many teens push their parents away, a little or a lot. It's part of the package. But it can be hard on moms and dads. So don't be *too* in-their-face about it.

Bette Davis said, "If you have never been hated by your child, you have never been a parent."

Perhaps. Yet while it's important to become your own person, don't go overboard with the "I hate you"s.

Peace at home is better for everybody.

Ups and downs may be all right—
But there really is no need to bite.

No matter how out-of-it your parents may seem to you,
they're still your parents.

−Dave Barry

E ven if your parents dress weird and say stupid stuff in front of your
friends, they're still your parents. You can't make them go away.

You probably wouldn't even want to.

After all, not only do they wash your clothes, make your dinner,
and provide clean sheets, but their love is *unconditional*. Meaning if
you screw up, they get disappointed, but they still love you. They
aren't fickle.

Friendships shift.

Relationships come and go.

Parents are for keeps.

At some point, when you're getting ready to glare at them, consider appreciating their one or two good points. Would you truly trade
them in for cooler parents? Would you honestly prefer parents who
dress as if they're ready for their *Teen People* closeup or reality TV
series? Or parents who never ask about your day or grades or who
never wait for you to come in at night?

Your parents may be busy—or bizarre—but they probably are not as
pathetic as you imagine.

(On the other hand, if you think your parents can do absolutely *no*
wrong, you'd also be . . . wrong.)

Your parents aren't perfect, but they're yours.

To understand your parents' love,
you must raise children yourself.
—CHINESE PROVERB

This is not to say you should rush right out there and reproduce. But switch camera angles for a second and look at how you act at home. Do you walk in, rush to your bedroom, slam your door, turn on your computer, blast your music, and stay out of sight until dinner has been prepared for you or until you emerge asking for money on your way back out? Are you smoking or cutting classes or going with someone years older or coming home hours late with bloodshot eyes?

I hope not. But no wonder some parents feel shut out or freaked out!

Picture yourself as a parent. How would you feel if your teenager rarely spoke to you or was flunking school or had a drawer full of pills?

"As soon as you become responsible for someone very very young, it suddenly makes you feel very very old," said writer John O'Farrell.

Raising kids is a huge job. If you make the job a little easier for your parents, they'll probably make life a little easier for you. And if you can bring yourself to say thanks for cooking a meal you like, washing your jeans, buying graph paper, carpool picking-up and dropping-off, packing lunches, planning vacations, or whatever, if you can express even a smidgen of gratitude, believe me, *they'll* be grateful.

Consider your parents' point of view.

Why do grownups quarrel so easily, so much,
and over the most idiotic things?

—anne frank

Now that I've urged you to appreciate those fogies who try to run your life, let me say that things can get loud in my home, too.

Quarreling happens. And it's usually about the stupidest stuff, like who ate the last Pop-Tart, who took the hairbrush, who forgot to put the cordless phone back, and who left water in the tub. While fussing is natural, nobody enjoys it.

Want to avoid fights? Here's how:

* ★ Keep your voice down.

* ★ Never say, "You don't get it," or "Everyone else . . ." because that pushes parental buttons.

* ★ Don't ask for cash when your parents are already stressed, grouchy, late, or in the shower.

* ★ If you messed up, say, "I'm sorry." Most parents stop screaming the second you choke out an apology.

* ★ If your parent is yelling at you but is really angry about something else, say something like, "Mom, you're mad at Dad, not me. Let's not fight, okay?" (Note: This works only on evolved parents.)

* ★ To end a quarrel, don't rush in with the last word. Try, "Point taken," or "I see what you mean," or "Okay."

One reason why family members sometimes say horrible things to one another is because they know that an hour later, they'll all be passing the ketchup as though nothing ever happened.

But as John Lennon sang, "Give peace a chance."

You can stop the fighting.

All that I am or hope to be I owe to my mother.

—aBraHam LINcoLN

I might sound dorky if your school president said that. But it's sort of sweet coming from one of our nation's presidents.

A few moms score high approval ratings from their kids. Many more seem embarrassing or distant or overprotective or pushy.

But most moms mean well. Did your mom start cheering (loudly or softly) for you from Day One? Even if the woman you call "Mom" entered the picture later, she's probably there for you now.

That's not nothing.

"There was a point when I was thirteen and didn't really appreciate anyone's input, but I got over that. My mom's advice is priceless to me now," said Alexis Bledel, who plays Rory on *Gilmore Girls*.

"The doctors told me I would never walk, but my mother told me I would—so I believed my mother," said Wilma Rudolph, U.S. Olympic gold medalist.

If your mother is your biggest fan, count your blessings and be her fan, too. She deserves it!

If not, can you find other adults who believe in you and are rooting for you? You deserve it!

What has your mom done for you?
What have you done for her?

There must always be a struggle between a father and son,
while one aims at power and the other at independence.

—Samuel Johnson

The road from dependence to independence is a rocky one. Sons and daughters fight with fathers and mothers.

You're testing yourself, and while you're at it, you're testing them. They'd probably *like* to pass the test, but probably fail fairly often.

Just as it's fun and hard to be a teen, it's fun and hard to be a parent of a teen.

The thing is, even if your dad is gruff, he's still on your side. He wants you to grow up—just not too fast.

Some dads actually say, "I love you."

Others express love by ordering pepperoni pizza (your favorite) instead of anchovy and onion pizza (their favorite). Or by taking you to early morning Saturday games instead of sleeping in and reading the paper cover to cover.

Others show they care by getting on your case to study harder, clean your room, practice your trumpet, finish your salad, or improve your running time.

Some are overprotective; some give almost too much space. Some dads are distant because their dads were distant. Maybe yours is doing his best and needs you to be the one to suggest an afternoon of fishing or a night at the movies.

Whatever your dad's style, you can be sure that other teens have fathers, or situations, like yours.

If your father is proud, prove him right. If not, prove him wrong!

My father didn't give attention to me as a kid. It's one of those things that I'm still dealing with and trying to get through.

—Janet Jackson

Some dads and moms seem to be missing in action. Others are literally out of the picture.

"I like to believe I was an immaculate conception, but unfortunately, my mother says no," said actress Sarah Michelle Gellar. Novelist John Irving said he has no desire to track down his absentee dad: "I haven't lost a night's sleep thinking about him."

If your mother or father is around but not around, or is alive but you haven't heard from that parent for years, this is their loss as well as yours.

Maybe you're used to the situation and it's not that big a deal. Or maybe you realize that you're actually better off without this parent.

"The only thing you can rely on about your father," Cher told Winona Ryder in Patty Dann's *Mermaids,* "is that he can't be relied on."

It's best not to idolize a missing parent or imagine a talk show reunion. If possible, accept that you've been managing without for a while and can continue doing so. Recognize that the parent's absence (physical, emotional, or both) is not your fault. And try to find other adults who would love to be a part of your life.

Finally, think about these words from a Lois Lowry novel: "Take pride in your pain. You are stronger than those who have none."

From pain, strength.

Children should be born without parents.

—Langston Hughes

 ome parents are hypercritical. Some remind you not to say *like* every two seconds, not to eat with your fingers, not to lean back in your chair, and not to start a dirty underwear collection on the floor of your closet.

In your most lucid moments, you can see that they do this for *your* own sake. But it still gets old.

What to do? Talk to them about it. And talk to *yourself* about speech, table manners, and closet cleaning.

The more you push yourself, the less they'll need to push you.

Realize, too, that some individuals simply aren't natural-born parents. Some compare you with your brother the scholar-athlete. Some insist on giving you a hug right outside school. Some complain about your grades when you think you deserve praise. And some spend so much time with their new love or new kids that they forget that you still need some one-on-one time, too.

Let your parents know when you feel embarrassed or unappreciated. Tell them where it hurts. Instead of flopping on your bed and saying, "You wouldn't understand!" explain it. Say, "Mom, if you have to hug me, do it in the kitchen, not at the bus stop." Or "Dad, when I spend the weekend with you and Suzie and your baby, we hardly get to talk. Could we go out to lunch this Saturday, just us?"

Tell them how you feel. They'd rather love you than torture you.

Parents don't mean to be mean.

We all have to learn to accept people for who they are and not who we want them to be.

—terry mcmillan

L inda and Paul McCartney said that all they wanted for their four children "was for them to have big hearts." Do your parents want you to be compassionate? Happy? Successful? All of the above? Do they expect too much? Too little? Do they push just the right amount?

Probably not. No parent gets it exactly right. But you *can* talk to them about their goals for you versus your goals for yourself.

Just as parents should accept kids for who they are, kids should try to accept parents for who they are. Maybe yours are not terrific role models. Maybe they never ask about games, or auditions, or homework. Or maybe you're the one who never talks to them about what matters to you.

You know how TV shows often end with insights, hugs, swelling music, and canned guffaws?

Well, that's TV, not real life.

In real life, It usually takes a lot more than thirty minutes to unravel long-standing arguments. In real life, people have shortcomings. And in real life, there's no laugh track. (Thank God. I *hate* laugh tracks.)

If your home life is a struggle, have faith that things may improve, and remind yourself that you won't live at home forever. But also give your parents a break. If you are less quick to get mad at them or make fun of them or ignore them, they may turn nicer before your very eyes. Think about how *you* can change your situation or attitude instead of just wishing *they* would change theirs.

Be patient with your parents.

It was odd how one found oneself making trivial conversation
on important occasions. Perhaps it was because one
could not say what was really in one's mind.

—Barbara Pym

If you're upset about a test or performance or summer plan, talk about it. If you need to break some news to your parents, try, "This is awkward but there's something I want to tell you."

Looking for advice? Say, "I want to ask you something, but please don't make light of it. This is hard for me and I want to be able to talk to you about personal stuff." If you give parents that kind of warning, you're setting the stage for a genuine heart-to-heart (or at least mouth-to-ears).

Sometimes the best conversations happen in cars or on telephones or online or during evening walks or at bedtime when the lights are out. Eye contact is ideal, but people sometimes communicate best when there is no eye contact.

Like kids, many parents get nervous about broaching tricky topics. Help one another out.

Nobody ever died from feeling awkward.

Small talk is okay; real talk is better.

Is solace anywhere more comforting than in the arms of sisters?
—alice walker

I wasn't lucky enough to grow up with a sister.

For a guy, a sister may offer insights about women, and an instant "in" with a lot of girls.

For a girl, a sister may offer the chance to share clothes, jewelry, makeup (she'll share back), as well as girl talk and laughter. (But stay away from each other's crushes or boyfriends.)

Either way, a sister can be a lifelong confidante.

Virginia Woolf wrote, "Dear Sister, You cannot think how I depend on you, and when you're not there, the color goes out of my life."

Tennis champion Serena Williams said, "I just want to thank Venus for supporting me all the way, and just being the best sister in the whole world."

If you and your sister quarrel nonstop, can you try a truce? Can you try to be teammates instead of rivals? Consider this poem by Ella Wheeler Wilcox:

We flatter those we scarcely know
We please the fleeting guest,
And deal full many a thoughtless blow
To those who love us best.

Turn siblings into friends.

You should never do anything wicked and lay it on your brother, when it is just as convenient to lay it on some other boy.

—mark twain

I f you have a brother but all you do is put each other down, at least you're toughening each other up and giving yourselves bounce-back skills. But can't you try a cease-fire? You'd both come out ahead.

Rather than compare yourself with your brother, work on your strengths. Rather than criticize him, shock him with a compliment. If he's down about something, give him a pep talk or send an encouraging e-mail. If he's the one picking fights, say, "I don't want to argue." If he's older, seek his advice or homework help. Try being honest with each other. If he's younger and a tagalong, give him some undivided attention (a quick game of Crazy Eights won't kill you), and explain that afterward you'll need to be alone. Then tell yourself that while it's hard to be spied on or followed, your brother is not going to be five forever. (Blink twice, and he may be your size or, God forbid, taller!) So boost him up, don't belittle him. You're looking at a future friend—not to mention your future children's uncle!

I have two older brothers. We squabbled as kids, and sometimes still do. We also got along, and still do! One thing for sure: There are far more group-hug photos of them in my scrapbooks than of my high school boyfriends or college pals.

Friends come and go, but family is always there. (If you have no siblings, think about which cousins or close friends can become almost-siblings.)

When siblings fight, everyone loses.

*One of the luckiest things that can happen to you in life
is to have a happy childhood.*

—agatha christie

I agree with Agatha, but here's what another mystery writer, Sue Grafton, said: "One of my theories is that no one with a happy childhood ever amounts to much in this world. They are so well adjusted, they never are driven to achieve anything."

You cannot choose whether you'll have a "happy childhood" any more than you can choose your parents. You *can* make the most of your situation and be an achiever no matter what your background. As Oprah Winfrey said, "Don't let a bad childhood stand in your way."

Maybe you have devoted parents who guide you from one fine school to the next and provide money and culture as you prepare to spread your wings and soar.

Or maybe you have difficult parents, and perhaps financial troubles, and you've had to keep track of your own schooling and seek out scholarships and wade your way into your future. Can you find a silver lining? Those who don't expect things to be handed to them can become extra resourceful and motivated.

There are many famous people (such as George W. Bush and Gwyneth Paltrow) who had famous fathers or mothers. There are many other famous people (such as Bill Clinton and Oprah) who had humbler beginnings and started almost from scratch.

Booker T. Washington said, "Success is to be measured not so much by the position that one has reached in life as by the obstacles that he has overcome while trying to succeed."

Your childhood, your springboard.

Yes, the past can hurt, but the way I see it,
you either run from it, or learn from it.
—Rafiki in *The Lion King*

D oes your home life hurt?
If you are being abused, should you tell?

How bad is the abuse? Is it emotional or physical? Will telling help protect you or your siblings? In how many years will you be out of your home and on your own anyway?

Your mom once called you a name or slapped you hard across the cheek? That stinks but that is not a call to action. Stay out of her way when she's upset, and perhaps talk to her or your dad about it at a quiet moment.

Your dad frequently leaves you black and blue? That is unacceptable and it's important that you know that you can change your situation. Confide in a relative or trusted adult. Or talk to a school counselor or health teacher—they're trained to listen and know how to get help if necessary. Or call a hot line (such as 1-800-HIT-HOME) and seek advice without giving your name and without its showing up on your phone bill. In an emergency, get immediate help by calling 911.

Nobody's family is perfect or perfectly loving. But if you feel unsafe in your home, you can do something about it. Life may feel worse in the short run—but better in the long run.

Remember in *The Wizard of Oz* when Dorothy splashes the Wicked Witch of the West with water? The Witch starts melting, m-e-l-t-i-n-g, and says, "Who ever thought a little girl like you could destroy my beautiful wickedness?" Girl or guy, little or big, you really do have the power to fight back.

When necessary, you can take control.

I might have been a goldfish in a glass bowl for

all the privacy I got.

—H. H. Munro

If your parents ransack your drawers, open your mail, listen in on phone calls, check your e-mail, read your journal, and never knock, then I wish *they* were reading this book so I could tell them to back off.

But since *your* eyes are on this page, here's some advice.

1. If you keep a journal, hide it well, lock it up, or use code. My parents never read my diaries and I'm glad they didn't, because keeping a diary helped me find my voice as a writer.

2. If you go online, have your own secret password and memorize it, or use an account that you set up yourself.

3. Don't have double standards: No opening parents' mail or barging into their room or checking their purse or briefcase.

4. Let them meet your friends—especially the polite ones who are sure to make a good impression.

5. If your parents ask, "Where are you going?" don't say, "Out." If you tell them what you're up to, they may not become so curious that they feel driven to snoop or eavesdrop.

6. Realize that they love you and they get paranoid because they know the world isn't 100 percent safe.

7. Tell your parents they have done a great job raising a trustworthy kid and they should relax and trust you. (Then don't give them a reason to stop trusting you.)

Keep earning your parents' trust.

Seeing a shrink is like jury duty. You can put if off for a few years,
but you gotta show up sooner or later.

—Rob ackerman

I confess. Rob Ackerman is my husband, and that's a line from a play he wrote.

Not everyone seeks therapy. But many people do. And many should.

If you feel not just down or upset (normal) or moody and angry (normal), but out of whack, lost, in despair, or suicidal, a trained professional can help you get back on track. It doesn't have to take years. And depending on insurance and local programs, it may not cost much. (Talking to a school counselor is free, and if you get a referral from a hospital or university psychology department, fees can be very reasonable.)

Besides, investing in yourself and your mental health can be the best time and money you ever spent. You pay to keep your hair in good shape. Why not your psyche?

Is every therapist brilliant? No. You may even have to shop around for the right person and right fit. But a good shrink can help you figure out which difficulties to accept and which to try to change. A good shrink can help you reclaim your confidence and go for your goals. And a good psychiatrist can, when necessary, prescribe medication.

If you do see a therapist or join a support group, talk. Don't just sit there waiting for magic to happen. Whether your issues are family-related or purely personal, shrinks and support groups have heard it all. They are there to listen and help—not to judge.

If you lose your balance, therapy can help get it back.

Family faces are magic mirrors. Looking at people who belong to us, we see the past, present, and future.

—gail lumet BUCKLEY

Let's hear it for extended families! Your second cousins and great-aunt and cute little nephews. Here's to reunions and shared vacations and crowded holiday tables.

Sure, it's natural to like some of your relatives more than others. But try not to hate any of them. "Hatred among kinsmen causes more grief than the stings of scorpions," wrote Ali, son-in-law of the prophet Muhammad. "If you judge people, you have no time to love them," said Mother Teresa.

You don't have to be best friends with all your relatives. And maybe your cousin is hopelessly out of touch with popular culture. Or maybe he or she is too into the latest trends or clothes or music and *you* could care less about all that. Or maybe your families do too much comparing and competing. Even so, sharing genes (as well as jeans) counts for a lot. In a crisis, families come through. They also offer continuity. You can count on them to be there at birthdays, graduations, weddings, and funerals.

If you and your cousins get together by a hearth in January or a bonfire in July, toast marshmallows and enjoy one another. You can find the fun of having a sibling without the taint of rivalry for parental attention.

Is your cousin already one of your best friends? How great is that? Have good times now and build memories for later.

Stay close to your cousins.

If I had my life to live over, I would have taken the time to
listen to my grandfather ramble about his youth.

—erma BOMBECK

Do your grandparents talk too much about politics or money or doctors? Instead of slinking away, draw them out on different subjects. Next time you're stuck at an endless birthday or December dinner, consider asking:

"Grandmom, what was the most trouble Mom ever got in?" "Did you punish her?" "What did you think of her first boyfriend?" "When did you meet Dad?"

"Granddad, what were you like when you were a kid?" "What were your grandparents like?" "Did you teach Dad to ride a bike?" "Where did you get married?" "Where did you honeymoon?"

Aunts and uncles can also fill you in on family folklore. Ask: "As a little sister, was Mom bratty, sweet, or both?" "Did you play tricks on each other?" "Did you like each other's friends?" "What were the best family vacations you ever had?" "Who were your favorite cousins growing up?"

You might even ask them for advice—which you can then take or leave. François de la Rochefoucauld wrote, "Old people love to give advice; it compensates them for their inability to set a bad example."

Sometimes older is wiser. Christopher Paul Curtis wrote at the end of *Bud, Not Buddy,* "Now I feel a real sorrow when I think of all the knowledge, wisdom, and stories that have been forever lost with the deaths of my grandparents."

Find your family's stories.

If you live to be a hundred, I want to live to be a hundred

minus one day, so I never have to live without you.

—a. a. milne's *Winnie the Pooh*

"The way to love anything is to realize that it may be lost," wrote British author G. K. Chesterton.

"We are children until our fathers die," wrote author Melissa Banks.

Many people are lucky enough to have their parents long after they themselves become parents.

Some of us aren't so lucky.

My father died when I was twenty-five. It blew a hole in my life, and for months all I did was fall in.

I cried a lot. I talked to a counselor. And I missed my father terribly. I kept expecting him to be cooking in the kitchen or setting up a game of Scrabble. Days and weeks and months went by and it just didn't seem possible that he was never going to walk in the door or wish me good-night.

While the loss of a parent lasts forever, the worst pain does not.

It's not that you ever really get over the death of a loved one, but you eventually come to terms with it, accept it. You have to. You have to keep living your own life.

Even though I have accepted my father's death, I don't think I ever actually "lost" him. He knew I loved him and I knew he loved me, so I like to imagine that in the important ways, he's still with me, safe and sound.

You don't forget loved ones who die. You take them with you.

As poet Seamus Heaney put it, "They're part of the light in your head."

Your family stays with you.

I don't reproach the spring for starting up again . . .
I know that my grief will not stop the green.
—WISLAWA SYMBORSKA

There is no right way to grieve. Some people cry; some don't. Some want to talk about it or write about it or draw about it; some don't. Some are stopped in their tracks; others become frenetic with activity.

"As long as I kept moving, my grief streamed out behind me like a swimmer's long hair in water. I knew the weight was there but it didn't touch me. Only when I stopped did the slick, dark stuff of it come floating around my face, catching my arms and throat til I began to drown. So I didn't stop," wrote Barbara Kingsolver in *The Poisonwood Bible* (which, by the way, is a great book).

No matter how a particular individual grieves, the world keeps on spinning. Seasons dare to follow seasons. Classmates continue flirting and gossiping and taking tests.

If you are grieving, you feel stranded. Be gentle with yourself. Allow yourself to feel terrible. But also give yourself permission to start your life back up again. To jump back onto the moving carousel. To feel better.

The person who died would not want your life to feel over. The person would want you to carry on. And perhaps to remember.

Pierce Brosnan, a.k.a. James Bond, said after his first wife died, "There's no escaping the pain. You have to sit in it, accept it, then you have to move out of it."

Mayor Rudy Giuliani said after the collapse of the World Trade Center buildings, "Those who were lost and missing would want us to continue. . . . Our hearts are broken, no question about that, but our hearts continue to beat, and they beat very, very strongly. Life is going to go on."

Time doesn't heal but it helps.

*There are two kinds of people in this world: those who have
known inescapable sorrow and those who have not.*

—Pearl S. Buck

O ne final page on this grim subject. (Skip if it's too much!)
If you are feeling flattened, be patient not only with yourself, but also
with those who want to comfort you and have no clue how. If a friend is
avoiding you or saying all the wrong things, say, "I just need you to listen." If a boyfriend or girlfriend does not have the right words, say, "Give
me a hug." If someone wants to talk, but at that moment you want to play
poker, say, "Thanks, but let's talk later, okay?" And if a classmate who
blew a math quiz moans, "This was the *worst* day of my life," quietly
remember that not everyone has your deeper perspective.

Grief sets you apart. But you are also not as alone as you think.
Others have mourned a death or survived the breakup of their family or
the horror of a disease or accident or disaster. Open up to a person who
has been there. Or ask a librarian for a book that might help, such as *A
Bridge to Terabithia* or *A Summer to Die* or *A Death in the Family* or *Death
Be Not Proud*.

If you know how devastating it is to feel your family come apart or
to lose someone or feel lost yourself, you may know how to comfort
someone in a similar situation. When it's your turn to reach out, you
probably won't be aloof or tongue-tied. You won't say, "I know exactly
how you feel," since no one can know exactly what someone else feels.
Instead, you might quietly ask, "How *are* you?" Even if it is awkward,
even if it is hard.

Learn how to seek comfort and give comfort.

Happiness is just a dog sunning itself.

—Samuel Taylor Coleridge

S ometimes a dog wagging its tail is the best welcome home a person could wish for. If you're sick in bed, having a cat to keep you company makes the day a whole lot brighter.

Do you have dogs, cats, birds, guinea pigs, fish, hamsters, gerbils, snakes, rabbits, toads, geckos, frogs, ferrets, an ant farm, or multiplying mice?

(We have pet mice. More by the month. Mama mouse is always preggers.)

If you have a pet, consider yourself lucky. Not only are most pets pettable (a word that is not in the dictionary but should be), but having a pet actually reduces stress.

George Eliot said, "Animals are such agreeable friends—they ask no questions, they pass no criticisms."

Penelope Cruz said she likes pets more than people because, "I don't have to argue with them." No argument there.

Pets can be family members, too.

But you knew that, right?

Love your pets and they'll love you.

Phone home.

−ℇ.ℑ.

In Stephen Spielberg and Melissa Mathison's masterpiece, E.T. misses his family so much that his heart glows red with yearning.

If you go away for the night or the weekend or the summer or the school year, stay in touch with your family. Pick up the phone, write a letter, send an e-mail.

Don't just disappear. You know how parents are. They worry. So reassure them that you're doing fine. And if you call when you're not fine—when you're upset or homesick—call again when you're feeling better.

Yes, no news is good news. But parents love to hear from kids.

Look at it this way. Your mom and/or dad held your fingers as you learned to toddle and pushed you in the playground swing and quizzed you on spelling words. They have loved you for as many years as you've been alive. C'mon. Are you sure you don't have a *minute* to check in from a pay phone or cell phone or friend's house?

E.T. missed his family when they were separated, and you'd miss yours. This is not to imply that you're a funny-looking alien or that you shouldn't sign up for adventure. It's just that, as Carol Shields wrote, "It takes people by surprise how much love they have stored up."

So go out there and conquer the world. But remember that, to your parents, you probably mean the world.

Touch base.

work

Your work is to discover your work and then
with all your heart give yourself to it.
−BUDDHA

What do you want to be when you grow up? Have people been asking you this ever since you were big enough to swing a bat?

"My work is my life," said actor Sir John Gielgud.

"Don't ever confuse the two, your life and your work," countered Pulitzer Prize–winner Anna Quindlen. "The second is only a part of the first."

She's right: *What* you are is not *who* you are. But your work is a big part of your life. Many adults spend more time working than playing. So it's important to like what you do Monday through Friday rather than just clock in the hours until Saturday and Sunday.

No one should stress out about the future. But do think ahead. Will you be an actor or athlete, doctor or lawyer, teacher or businessperson? Will you be a zookeeper, restaurant reviewer, or fashion designer? Perhaps a politician, personal trainer, police officer, or photographer . . . ?

"First say to yourself what you would be; and then do what you have to do," advised Greek philosopher Epictetus.

How can you get from here to there?

To love what you do and feel that it matters—
how could anything be more fun?
—Katherine Graham

S tart noticing which careers excite you, which seem satisfying, which pay well, which help the world, which do none of these, which do all.

When you think about your future, don't just picture yourself behind a desk, in front of a classroom, arguing before a jury, or singing for fans. Picture your work in the context of your life.

Notice that some jobs and careers are more accommodating, flexible, and family-friendly than others. Thinking about being a teacher? You're allowed to like the idea of summers off. Thinking about delivering babies or producing a talk show? You're allowed to recognize that your days might be exciting—but you might be on call even while asleep.

As a self-employed writer, I can work at home and make my own hours. I like that I can take an afternoon off—or work all weekend. Other people might prefer the camaraderie and structure provided by an office or school or store or factory.

What about you? Figuring out your future is a job in itself. Explore possibilities. Don't just grab whatever job is available; find work that fits your interests.

"It doesn't matter if it takes a long time getting there; the point is to have a destination," said writer Eudora Welty.

"If you can't do it with feeling, don't," advised singer Patsy Cline.

What kind of work would work for you?

You've got to be careful if you don't know where you're going
'cause you might not get there.
—YOGI BERRA

D on't worry if your future feels fuzzy. It's supposed to. The word *career* comes from the Latin for "road," and you should enjoy a long scenic drive.

"What I realized is that the question is the final answer. That what I wanted to do with my life is figure out what I wanted to do with my life," said writer Jonathan Safran Foer.

How do your parents make money? (Mine were writers, and we talked a lot about words and books.) Does their work appeal to you? How do their friends and your friends' parents make money? Do you get along with any adults or relatives whose work intrigues you? A vet? Baker? Editor? How did they get where they are? Can you ask to spend a day helping the person? Or a week as an intern? Can you get a summer job, paid or unpaid? You may love the work, or realize it's not for you. Either insight is valuable!

If possible, try several jobs as an employee or volunteer. Work at a restaurant, car repair shop, theater, or parent's office. Acquire different skills and spy on adults in action. Part of finding out what you want to do is finding out what you *don't* want to do.

Oprah Winfrey told a college audience that she grew up poor: "no electricity, the outhouse . . . the whole poor deal." She said that when she was four or five, "I was watching my grandmother outside boiling clothes and hanging them on the line, and she said, 'You better watch me now, girl, because someday you're going to have to know how to do this yourself.' And a little voice inside me said, 'No, Grandma.'"

Listen to the voice inside yourself.

If you always do what interests you,

at least one person is pleased.

—Katharine Hepburn

onfession: I did a lot better on my math SATs than on my English SATs. But I didn't love numbers the way I loved words. So I'm glad I've chosen a profession I'm passionate about.

J. K. Rowling's Professor Dumbledore said, "It is our choices, Harry, that show what we truly are, far more than our abilities."

If you're six feet six and can slam-dunk, but dislike basketball, you don't have to be a ballplayer. If you come from a family of grocers or dry cleaners or advertisers, but you love studying genomes or vaccines or dinosaur bones, you don't have to follow family footsteps. You can keep hanging out at the lab. Maybe you'll become a scientist—and maybe you should.

If you've always wanted to open a bookstore or work at an aquarium, start walking in that direction, even if you'd be terrific at any number of different jobs and your mother's heart was set on your becoming a heart surgeon.

Lots of people never experience joy on the job. "Oh, you hate your job?" asked Drew Carey. "Why didn't you say so? There's a support group for that. It's called EVERYBODY, and they meet at the bar."

There's no need to lock in your future yet. But be aware that the happiest people are the ones who like what they do, and who get better and better at it.

After winning the gold medal, Sarah Hughes, at age sixteen, said, "I skated for pure enjoyment. That's how I wanted my Olympic moment to be."

Don't just do what you do best. Do what you love most.

If you can dream it, you can do it.
—WALT DISNEY

"You have to have a dream so you can get up in the morning," said director Billy Wilder.

"Daydreaming is important," said children's book author and illustrator James Marshall. "I've practically made a career out of it."

Let your imagination run wild . . . then try to catch up with it. Chase your dreams. If you have the determination and discipline and talent to go with your dream, the future you envision may be within your grasp.

"I learned early," said Nobel Prize–winner Saul Bellow, "that a man can do anything he wishes to do, regardless of his age." A woman, too.

Okay, all right—maybe it *is* too late for you to become an Olympic skater, concert violinist, or pro football player—unless you're already a wunderkind. But otherwise, for you, the doors are open. And unless you screw up by flunking out of school or selling drugs, those doors will stay open for a while simply because you're young and full of potential.

Can you imagine where you might be in five or ten years?

While some dreams will not come true, others will exceed your expectations.

So if someone calls you a dreamer, that's fine.

As my friend Ed Abrahams said: The world needs dreamers.

Imagine.

Never try to catch two frogs with one hand.

*—*CHINESE PROVERB

W hile it's important to dream, it's also necessary (sigh) to be realistic.

If you're counting on winning a Grammy, an Oscar, *and* a Tony by age twenty-two, you're heading for disappointment.

Mind you, you should expect a lot of yourself. You should go for the gold. Sprinter Marion Jones said, "I do not come out here to race for silver."

But you also deserve the pleasure of experiencing success. So set goals that are attainable. If success is a stairway, think about climbing up, taking pride in each step, and not stopping in the middle.

My goal was to become a writer. When I reached that goal, I fine-tuned it: I wanted to become a novelist. It took me a bunch of decades, several false starts, and numerous rejection letters, but now I also write novels for kids. I'd still like to write a novel for adults—and I hope I will.

Notice that I didn't say that my goal is to have a number one best-seller. Making the list is not within my personal control. Writing the best books I can is.

Similarly, if you like to act, you're better off if your goal is to be a great actor, not a famous one. (Do I hope you'll become famous? Sure! But you'll want to enjoy your work whether or not you get worldwide acclaim.)

What are your short- and long-term aspirations? Can you take courses that would help you realize them? Can you meet potential mentors? Can you find a part-time job that could lead to a lifetime career?

Think about how to get where you're going, step by step by step.

Set the bar high—but not unreasonably high. Adjust as needed.

I believe in positive thinking—

and willing yourself to do things you think you can do.

—FreDDIe Prinze Jr.

I f you think you can do it, you probably can.

But it won't be a piece of cake.

It will require time and energy—and you've got that, right?

"I don't know that there are any short cuts to doing a good job," said Supreme Court Justice Sandra Day O'Connor.

"Opportunity is missed by most people because it is dressed in overalls and looks like work," said inventor Thomas Edison.

His work gave us the lightbulb.

What might yours give us?

It is not enough

To sit on your duff.

You know what they call the guy who finishes last
in medical school? They call him Doctor!
—abe Lemons

H ard work pays off. So does staying at it, persevering, hanging in
there, not giving up.

Consider Aesop's fable of the tortoise and the hare. The hare was quick but smug and took one nap too many. So the slow-and-steady tortoise—the laughable underdog—lumbered across the finish line first.

It's nice to win.

But it's crucial to start, keep going, and finish.

"You may be disappointed if you fail, but you are doomed if you don't try," said opera singer Beverly Sills.

"When you have a great and difficult task, something perhaps almost impossible, if you only work a little at a time, every day a little, suddenly the work will finish itself," wrote novelist Isak Dinesen.

Don't stop now.

It's so much easier to write a résumé than to craft a spirit.

—anna QUINDLEN

The shape of your spirit counts more than the shape of your résumé. But writing a résumé is a good exercise and often a necessary one. Can you try to express who you are by listing what you've done?

Your résumé should fit on one (one!) page and should include your name, address, phone number, and strengths. If you've been a lifeguard or camp counselor, say where and when. If you've volunteered at a church or synagogue or soup kitchen, say so. And if you're a star athlete or stellar student or lead actor, or if you know Japanese or HTML, point that out. Keep it short and simple—but this is no time for modesty.

Put your best foot forward, and show your résumé to your parents and teacher and maybe a friend before giving out any copies. Then save your résumé on a computer so you can update it often and easily. (Those tweaks and changes may even help you see your own career path more clearly.)

Your résumé allows potential employers (and perhaps college admissions officers) to learn in a glance what you've been up to and, most important to them, what you can bring to their table.

Saying who you are can help you see who you'll be.

Marge: Homer, the plant called. They said if you don't show up tomorrow, don't bother showing up on Monday.

Homer: Woo-hoo! Four day weekend!

—matt groening's *the simpsons*

O nce you say yes to a job, be it baby-sitting, tutoring, frying onion rings, filing at a law firm, or doing volunteer work, play by the rules.

★ **Arrive on time and alone.** Not with your friend or mom.

★ **Look the part.** What are other workers wearing? Running shoes? Suits? Tank tops? At work, you're supposed to look serious, not sexy, or as if you're ready for the gym.

★ **Make yourself useful.** If you spend every minute shadowing your boss and asking, "Now what should I do?" you'll become annoying. Find out what is expected of you, then do it, checking in only as needed.

★ **Sound secure.** Some people end all their sentences with a question mark? This is sweet but does not inspire confidence?

★ **Leave personal problems at home.** Be friendly, but don't show up fuming about your parents or weeping about your ex.

What if you *are* doing a masterful job making yourself indispensable? Congratulations! But don't let this work make you fall behind in your schoolwork.

In the big picture, getting through school counts more than, for instance, waiting tables. Eventually, you may want to have not just a job (a task for which you get paid), but a career (portable skills and a reputation). And while you can learn a lot waiting tables, you may not want to do that forever. So don't let the thrill of a paycheck distract you from the importance of a diploma.

Real work and schoolwork—both count.

One of the advantages of being disorderly is that one is constantly making exciting discoveries.

−a. a. milne

M y desk is usually a total utter disaster and I wish I could magically clean it up one-two-three like Harry Potter.

But I can't. Sometimes I do manage to straighten it up a bit, filing some papers, chucking others, paying a bill, answering a letter. But neat 'n' tidy has never been my strong suit, and even my virtual desktop fills up fast.

If you are naturally orderly and organized, I salute you.

If you aren't, from time to time, try, really try, to spruce up your cluttered desktop (or messy bedroom)—maybe with upbeat music blaring or a kitchen timer set for thirty minutes. Billy Collins wrote: "Clean the place as if the Pope were on his way." You will be glad you did, and your parents will, too—they may even offer to help!

Beyond that, hey, if you're getting your work done despite all appearances, go ahead and forgive yourself.

We all have different work habits and styles.

If it works for you, it works.

The best thing about being an artist is that you get to engage in satisfying work. Even if you never publish a word, you'll have something important to pour yourself into.

—anne lamott

A
re you creative?

"Without creativity, life is one long rerun," said TV writer Larry Gelbart.

If you have a talent, try not to take it for granted. Work on it. Develop it. Respect it. Stretch it. Flaunt it. Study it. Enjoy it. Take lessons. Practice.

Even Mozart had to practice. Sure, he was born with a gift. But Mozart had to learn scales before he could dazzle kings. What if he had decided he was too busy or too tired or too self-conscious to sit down and make music?

Don't take *your* talents for granted, either. Work on them. Enjoy them.

Polish pianist Ignacy Paderewski said, "If I don't practice one day, I know it. If I don't practice two days, my friends know it. If I don't practice three days, the whole world knows it."

"We can't take any credit for our talents. It's how we use them that counts," wrote novelist Madeleine L'Engle.

"If you have never been creative in your younger days, you must not expect to write, or paint, or compose music simply because you have grown old," wrote novelist Robertson Davies. "But if you have done these things when young, you will probably go on till you drop."

(Note to any trespassing adult readers: If the above quote seems discouraging because you've never been creative but are still secretly hoping for a retrospective at a museum or crowd at Lincoln Center, all I can say is #1, there's always hope, and #2, I warned you, this book is for teens.)

Express yourself!

I'm tough, ambitious, and I know exactly what I want. If that
makes me a bitch, okay.

–madonna

S ometimes you have to be a bitch to get things done," said Madonna, who also said, "I always thought I should be treated like a star."

Call me naive, but I think you can get what you want without being cocky or arrogant. You do, however, have to be assertive and persistent. And you have to imagine yourself succeeding.

Madonna is an example of someone who knew early on what she wanted and made it her business to get it.

(Some say *Bitch* stands for Babe In Total Control of Herself!)

Writer Maya Angelou once said: "I love to see a young girl go out and grab the world by the lapels." (Maybe a young guy, too.)

Be as zealous and ambitious as you want.

There is only one success—

to be able to spend your life in your own way.

—CHRISTOPHER MORLEY

The above quote is one of my very favorites. Success isn't about the biggest car or paycheck or bank account or about whether your name is known or dad is proud. It's about being happy. Feeling good about who you are and how you spend your time.

"Success is liking yourself, liking what you do, and liking how you do it," said Maya Angelou.

Might there come a time when you would say, "Yay! I'm successful! I did what I wanted to do and now I'm done," or "Hurray! I'm rich and famous—I think I'll quit"?

Maybe. But it's the journey that's interesting, not some imaginary finish line. That's why Carlos Santana didn't stop making music and Jay Leno didn't quit making jokes and Bill Gates didn't say, "Enough with the computers." It's also why Oprah and Madonna and other one-name powerhouses didn't get to the top, then announce their retirements.

The very successful George Bernard Shaw wrote, "I dread success. To have succeeded is to have finished one's business on earth, like the male spider, who is killed by the female the moment he has succeeded in his courtship. I like a state of continual becoming, with a goal in front and not behind."

If you could do anything, what would it be?

The person who says it cannot be done should not
interrupt the person doing it.
—CHINESE PROVERB

Some individuals' lot in life is to dream. Do your friends' dreams seem impossible? Let them discover this on their own rather than discourage them from going after what they want and then have them resent you if they fail to get there.

Besides, with luck, planning, and hard work, their lofty dreams may come true. Sometimes, as in Ruth Krauss and Crockett Johnson's *The Carrot Seed,* if you keep watering seeds, pulling weeds, and ignoring naysayers, giant carrots really *do* come up.

Let me add that as you yourself succeed, you'll run across people who are jealous or discouraging or who glom on to you when things are going well and disappear when you go through a rough patch.

"If you are successful, you will win false friends and true enemies," said Kent M. Keith. "Succeed anyway."

Mind your own work.

Striving for perfection is the greatest stopper there is. . . .
It's your excuse to yourself for not doing anything.
Instead, strive for excellence, doing your best.
—Sir Laurence Olivier

The people who win big prizes or make big money are still just people. Flawed and fallible human beings.

The masterpieces of our time, the best novels, the best movies, the best music, the best websites, the best sculptures, still have weaknesses and fault lines. There is always room for improvement.

But so what? Wouldn't we rather take them as they are than not at all?

Every single painting by Rembrandt, poem by Edna St. Vincent Millay, and song by the Beatles is not absolutely perfect. But I, for one, am glad that Rembrandt, Edna, John, Paul, George, and Ringo worked as hard as they did and didn't get tripped up in a quest for perfection.

Many of us are perfectionists, but none of us is perfect. So don't aim for perfection. Aim for excellence—and get the job done.

Do your best—even if it's not the best.

Work is the nearest thing to happiness that I can find.

—Zora Neale Hurston

You know how sometimes you wish you'd said something but the moment has passed, so then you have to just let it go?

Recently a college friend asked about my work, and I said I was about to start *With Love from Spain, Melanie Martin*. She knows I used to live in Spain and that this would be the third book in my travel diary series.

"You'll be able to write that in your sleep!" she chimed.

She smiled and I smiled, but somehow the comment annoyed me.

She hadn't meant it meanly. But I wish I'd said: "Why would I write a book I could write in my sleep?"

After all, books take time to write, and not only do I *not* want to bore you, dear reader, but I don't want to bore myself! You invest hours or days in my book; I invest months, years.

If you like five hundred–piece jigsaw puzzles, you wouldn't get excited about a fifty-piece puzzle, right? What's fun about doing something too easy? Nothing.

Hard work may have a bad name, but we *want* to be challenged. "The struggle alone teaches us, not the victory," said French writer Blaise Pascal.

"Work could cure almost anything," wrote Ernest Hemingway.

Here's hoping your work is hard enough so that it's not boring, but not *so* hard that it's intimidating. Every job has boring sides and boring days. But you're lucky if you can't do your work in your sleep.

Even pilots shouldn't just go on automatic pilot.

Life is what we make it, always has been, always will be.
—grandma moses

Maybe you're bussing tables this summer, or maybe, just maybe, bussing tables will be your forever job.

Not everyone wants to or can own the restaurant or be the maître d' or award-winning chef.

Let me tell you something: It's important to take pride in what you *are* doing. Sure, you can (and should) think about getting to the next step on the stairway of success, especially while you're young. But you can (and should) also enjoy where you are right now. If you are bussing tables, you can have fun doing it—or you can be zombielike as you trade time for money. The choice is yours.

Many teens and adults have jobs they don't love but do need because food, shelter, clothing, and medicine cost money. Well, it's better to find the good in that job than to curse fate 24/7.

You know how some cashiers look through you as they hand you your change? You know how others meet your eyes and smile and joke and seem to *mean* it when they wish you a nice day?

Guess which ones are having a better time at work and life?

Martin Luther King Jr. said, "If a man is called a streetsweeper, he should sweep streets even as Michelangelo painted, or Beethoven composed music, or Shakespeare wrote poetry. He should sweep streets so well that all the hosts of heaven and earth will pause to say, Here lived a great streetsweeper who did his job well."

Take pride in your work.

Strength does not come from winning. Your struggles develop your strengths. When you go through hardships and decide not to surrender, that is strength
—arnold schwarzenegger

Will there be setbacks?
Yes.

But try not to let them set you back very far.

Listen to your family or friends or loved one or coach or teachers—whoever gives the best pep talks. Read inspiring books; listen to motivational tapes; recall some of your triumphs; do whatever it takes to get yourself revved up again.

Then get back in the game.

"Never never never give up," said Winston Churchill.

"It's not whether you get knocked down; it's whether you get up," said football coach Vince Lombardi.

Actress Sandra Bullock said, "Praise gets me nowhere. Rejection makes me better myself. I don't go, 'Oh God, someone said I suck, and now I'm going to quit.' I can't quit. It's not something that knocks me down."

Uh-oh. Now I'm debating with myself. Do I leave this upbeat page alone? Or do I add the sad truth that sometimes it makes sense to quit while you're behind? For instance, if you want to be a model, but you've gone on two hundred go-sees without landing a single callback (let alone photo shoot), you may want to use your time in other ways. As W. C. Fields said, "If at first you don't succeed, try again. Then quit. No use being a damn fool about it."

Or as Milton Berle put it, "If at first you don't succeed, your skydiving days are over!"

Don't give up—get up!

Slump? I ain't in no slump . . .

I just ain't hitting.

−Yogi Berra

Everybody loses from time to time. What's bad is if you start thinking you're a loser.

Hang on to your winning attitude even if you aren't winning the games or prizes or tournaments.

Coach Vince Lombardi got it right when he said, "Confidence is contagious. So is lack of confidence." Try to tune out the friends, teammates, or family members who always sound defeatist.

If you think you'll bomb the test, come in last, get stage fright, or feel homesick, you just might. Many people with low expectations wind up living up (down) to them.

On the other hand, if you think you'll ace the test, win the race, knock 'em dead, and have a blast . . . you just might.

As Christopher Morley wrote, "Big shots are only little shots who keep shooting."

You can *turn things around for yourself.*

Worry is a word that I don't allow myself to use.

—DWIGHT D. EISENHOWER

Maybe you have a big baseball game coming up. Or performance. Or date. Or interview. Or maybe tomorrow is the first day at a new job.

You've been looking forward to this moment.

Are you nervous? Scared? Panicked?

Don't be. Tell yourself you're excited, not scared. You've worked hard for this, you've earned it, and you're ready! As the lead actor in the drama of your life, you are entitled to take center stage and shine.

I was on the *Today* show, and I'll confess that when I sat in the hot seat next to Katie Couric (!!!!), and we started talking (!!!!), live (!!!!), before millions of viewers (!!!!), well, the butterflies in my stomach began flying every which way and crashing into each other.

Yet, I had hoped for this moment. And I wasn't winging it—I had practiced. Afterward, my mother-in-law asked, "How could you think of all that off the top of your head?" Top of my head?! I'd spent days wandering around muttering to myself, "Well, Katie, that's exactly right . . ." precisely so that when we were on the air, I would look cool, calm, and confident. I had prepared, so instead of thinking, "Omigod omigod omigod," I was silently saying, *This is so cool! I've dreamed of this and worked for this and now, here I am. YESSSSSS!*

Next time you're exactly where you want to be (singing onstage or making a speech, or talking with someone special), encourage yourself to feel lucky and deserving and grateful—not jittery and inadequate and frightened.

Is this a crisis—or an opportunity?

Money is the root of all evil, and yet it is such a useful root
that we cannot get on without it any more than
we can without potatoes.

—LOUISA MAY ALCOTT

Timothy in the Bible said, "Love of money is the root of all evil;" George Bernard Shaw countered, "Lack of money is the root of all evil."

Woody Allen said, "Money is better than poverty, if only for financial reasons."

What *everyone* agrees upon is that we need the stuff.

Ogden Nash wrote:

Certainly there are lots of things in life that
money won't buy,
but it's very funny—
Have you ever tried to buy them
without money?

If you're an heir or heiress and already rock-star rich, lucky you! Otherwise, if you know how to spend money, you'd better learn how to earn it. For now, that may mean baby-sitting, mowing lawns, tutoring, taking care of a neighbor's child or pet, teaching computer skills (maybe even to a grandparent?), doing extra household chores, having a garage or sidewalk sale, helping at a party, or painting a neighbor's garage. Put up some notices and your phone may start ringing.

Consider these words of Whoopi Goldberg: "The greatest thing I was ever able to do was give a welfare check back saying, 'Here, I don't need this anymore.'"

Money matters.

You can be young without money but you can't be old without it.
—tennessee williams

When I traveled to Europe as a teenager, I stayed at hostels, campsites, and budget pensions. I'd earned lots of dollars as a baby-sitter and cashier, and I made that money last. I roughed it and loved it.

If you live for designer clothes, lavish gifts, and filet mignon, if you think the only way to go to the prom is by limo, you (or *someone* behind you) may have to spend a lot of hours working just so you can live in luxury.

Hey. You're young. You can have a great time for cheap—or free. Take a picnic to a free outdoor concert. Visit art galleries. Go hiking. Check newspapers and websites to see what's going on near you.

Stretch your dollars. Don't hoard your cash, but learn to shop for sales and find discounts and eat at less pricey restaurants. You can have rich experiences without blowing your budget. And you can have enough money to meet all your needs—"needs," not "greeds."

You'll be doing yourself a favor if you get in the habit of saving us well as spending. Later, if you earn more, you can spend more. Oh, and when banks start offering you credit cards, be careful. When you buy with plastic, it's not free—you get extra time to pay the bill, yes, but you may have to pay a little extra, too. So don't shop with money you don't have.

Take care of your money and your money
will take care of you.

I do want to get rich but I never want to do
what there is to do to get rich.

—Gertrude Stein

F. Scott Fitzgerald said, "The rich are different from us." Ernest Hemingway replied, "Yes, they have more money."

If you want to get rich and you're okay with doing whatever it takes to get there (sacrifice, long hours), more power to you. If you can figure out a fun way of making pots of money, even better!

But remember that piling up money does not have to be your master plan.

Joseph Campbell wrote, "If you follow your bliss, you will always have your bliss, money or not. If you follow money, you may lose it, and you will have nothing."

Lao-Tse wrote, "He who is content is wealthy."

Right now, while you're in school, learning is your real priority. Homework is your work.

Soon enough you'll have rent and taxes to pay, so take advantage of the free ride while it lasts.

Later, when you have to make a living, I hope you'll do what it takes to have a career that is both satisfying and lucrative. But I also hope you won't be so driven that you'll forget to smell the roses along the way— not to mention the hyacinths and orange blossoms.

After all, while the bottom line is important, so is the rest of the page.

And as James Thurber quipped, "It is better to have loafed and lost, than never to have loafed at all."

Life is to be savored.

END QUOTES

mindbodyfriendsrelationshipsschoolfamilyworkquotesad

As with the first dozen lines that started this book, these last forty-two lines stand on their own. Why not add your own favorites? This isn't just my book, it's yours. I hope you'll refer to it when you need a quote for a report or yearbook or toast. Or when you need a second, third, or fourth opinion from a poet, painter, or president. Or when you just want to mull things over or consider things from a new angle. ("The early bird gets the worm" is a proverb "—but the second mouse gets the cheese" is an add-on.)

By the way, if you want to keep all these quotes and the ones that precede them at your fingertips, follow the advice in the very next sentence!

Never lend books, for no one ever returns them.
The only books I have in my library are books
that other folks have lent me.
—anatole france

My mother groaned! My father wept.
Into the dangerous world I leapt!
—william blake

What if the Hokey Pokey is what it's all about?
—anonymous

I can accept failure. Everyone fails at something.
But I can't accept not trying.
—michael jordan

I am beginning to learn that it is the sweet,
simple things of life which are the real ones after all.
—Laura Ingalls Wilder

One is never as fortunate or as unfortunate as one imagines.
—François De La Rochefoucauld

About all you can do in life is be who you are.
Some people will love you for you. Most will love you for what
you can do for them. And some won't like you at all.
—Rita Mae Brown

The U.S. Constitution doesn't guarantee happiness,
only the pursuit of it.
—Ben Franklin

Protect me from what I want.
—Jenny Holzer

Floating upward through a confusion of dreams and memory,
curving like a trout through the rings of previous risings, I surface.
My eyes open. I am awake.
—Wallace Stegner

And the day came when the risk to remain in the bud was more
painful than the risk it took to blossom.
—Anaïs Nin

What if there were no hypothetical questions?
—anonymous

*I can honestly say that I was never affected by the success
of an undertaking. If I felt it was the right thing to do,
I was for it regardless of the possible outcome.*
—Golda Meir

The philosophers are right: If it's not one thing, it's another.
—Preston Sturges

I am an artist. I am here to live out loud.
—Émile Zola

There is no truth, only perception.
—Gustave Flaubert

The truth is rarely pure and never simple.
—Oscar Wilde

*The power of accurate observation is commonly called cynicism
by those who have not got it.*
—George Bernard Shaw

*I never tried to prove anything to someone else.
I wanted to prove something to myself.*
—Kobe Bryant

*If you send up a weather vane or put your thumb in the air
every time you want to go do something different, to find out
what people are going to think about it, you're going to
limit yourself. That's a very strange way to live.*

—Jessye Norman

*Aim at a high mark and you will hit it. No, not the first time,
not the second time, and maybe not the third.
But keep on aiming and keep on shooting,
for only practice will make you perfect.
Finally, you'll hit the bull's-eye of success.*

—Annie Oakley

Put all your eggs in one basket—and Watch That Basket!

—Mark Twain

*I have made my world and it is a much better world than
I ever saw outside.*

—Louise Nevelson

I'm not confused. I'm just well-mixed.

—Robert Frost

*I don't want to get to the end of my life and
find that I just lived the length of it. I want to have lived
the width of it as well.*

—Diane Ackerman

The battles that count aren't the ones for gold medals.
The struggles within yourself—the invisible, inevitable battles
inside all of us—that's where it's at.
—Jesse Owens

Everyone who got where he is had to begin where he was.
—Robert Louis Stevenson

Just don't play it safe. You haven't, have you?
—Ernest Hemingway

When I found I had crossed that line,
I looked at my hands to see if I was the same person.
There was such a glory over everything.
—Harriet Tubman

Always continue the climb.
—Oprah Winfrey

The seed for nirvana exists in all of us.
The time has come to think more wisely, hasn't it?
—The Dalai Lama

Do not seek to follow in the footsteps of the wise.
Seek what they sought.
—Basho

Be wiser than other people if you can, but do not tell them so.
—Lord Chesterfield

Learning without wisdom is a load of books on a donkey's back.

—zora neale Hurston

We are powerful because we have survived.

—auDre LorDe

Our greatest glory is not in never falling,
but in rising every time we fall.

—COnFUCIUS

The end is nothing. The road is all.

—WILLa CatHer

Doesn't everyone want to celebrate something at
the end of the day?

—a. r. gUrneY

It's a funny old world. A man's lucky if he gets out alive.

—W. C. FIeLDS

Life isn't fair. It's just fairer than death, that's all.

—WILLIam goLDman

It would be ungracious to grumble.

—marY CaSSatt

My goodness how the time has flown.
How did it get so late so soon?

—Dr. SeUSS

INDEX

mindbodyfriendsrelationshipsschoolfamilywor

If you have any doubts that we live in a society controlled by men, try reading down the index of contributors to a volume of quotations, looking for women's names.

—elaine gill

O ld quotation books are filled with men's words. I tried to fill this one with the voices of men and women. Things are changing—slowly, slowly.

Abrahams, Ed, 209

Ackerman, Diane, 234

Ackerman, Elizabeth, 126

Ackerman, Emme, 126

Ackerman, Rob, 194

Adams, Henry, 147

Adler, Freda, 125

Aesop, 70

Affleck, Ben, 58

Albee, Edward, 17, 106, 108, 139

Alcott, Louisa May, 112, 226

Ali, 195

Ali, Muhammad, 90

Alice (*Alice in Wonderland* character), 11

Allen, Woody, 14, 22, 131, 165, 226

Altman, Aaron (*Broadcast News* character), 114

Amos, Tori, 125

Anderson, Margaret, 3

Anderson, Marian, 26

Angelou, Maya, 15, 69, 217, 218

Aniston, Jennifer, 55

Anonymous quotes, 4, 231, 233

Aristotle, 153

Armstrong, Louis, 89

Atticus (*To Kill a Mockingbird* character), 83

Atwood, Margaret, 17

Augustine, Saint, 104

Ausubel, Anna, 126

Ausubel, Johnny, 126

Bacon, Francis, Lord, 74

Baldwin, James, 99

Ball, Lucille, 101

Balzac, Honoré de, 78

Banks, Melissa, 197

Banks, Tyra, 54, 103

Barca, Pedro Calderón de la, 104

Barry, Dave, 42, 180

Barrymore, Drew, 66

Basho, 235

Beatles, 65

Belkin, Lisa, 77

Bell, "Cool Papa," 164

Belle (*Beauty and the Beast* character), 112

Bellow, Saul, 209

Berger, Sally, 86

Bergman, Ingrid, 121

Berle, Milton, 223

Berlin, Irving, 88

Berra, Yogi, 3, 69, 207, 224

Berry, Halle, 27, 145

Bert (*Mary Poppins* character), 117

Bethune, Mary McLeod, 29

Bible, the, 71

  Song of Solomon, 130

  Timothy, 226

Binoche, Juliette, 162

Bird, Matt, 126

Blair, Tony, 23, 82

Blake, William, 39, 231

Bledel, Alexis, 183

Bombeck, Erma, 44, 196

Borges, Jorge, 172

Brautigan, Richard, inside back cover

Brewster, Kingman, 148

Brontë, Charlotte, 90

Brooks, Mel, 41

Brosnan, Pierce, 198

Brown, Helen Gurley, 79

Brown, Rita Mae, 232

Bryant, Kobe, 233

Buck, Pearl S., 118, 199

Buckley, Gail Lumet, 195

Buddha, 205

Bullock, Sandra, 38, 55, 101, 223

Burgess, Anthony, 49

Burnett, Thomas, Jr., 23

Burstyn, Ellen, 118

Bushnell, Candace, 111

Campbell, Joseph, 10, 228

Carey, Drew, 208

Carey, Mariah, 124

Carlin, George, 14

Carroll, Lewis, 11

Carter, Graydon, 154

Casals, Pablo, 9

Cassatt, Mary, 236

Castaneda, Carlos, 14

Caterpillar (*Alice in Wonderland* character),
  11

Cather, Willa, 236

Cervantes, Miguel de, 47, 109

Chabon, Michael, 69

Cher, 138, 185

Chesterfield, Lord, 235

Chesterton, G. K., 197

Child, Julia, 62

Christie, Agatha, 191

Churchill, Winston, 158, 223

Cleary, Beverly, 156

Cline, Patsy, 206

Clinton, Hillary Rodham, 50

Cobb, Ty, 65

Coleridge, Samuel Taylor, 200

Colette, 15, 17

Collins, Billy, 147, 215

Confucius, 236

Costanza, George (*Seinfeld* character), 137

Coward, Noel, 178

Cowper, William, 41

Creech, Sharon, 95

Cruise, Tom, 67

Cruz, Penelope, 200

Crystal, Billy, 38

Cummings, E. E., 10

Cunningham, Michael, 154

Curtis, Christopher Paul, 196

Dahl, Roald, 155

Dalai Lama, the, 3, 28, 167, 235

Dann, Patty, 185

Danziger, Paula, 149

Dave Matthews Band, 65

Davies, Robertson, 216

Davis, Bette, 179

Dement, William, 48

Democritus, 68
Diaz, Cameron, 40, 58
Dickens, Charles, 13, 120
Didion, Joan, 156
Dietrich, Marlene, 133
Dillard, Annie, 17, 18, 150
Dinesen, Isak, 212
Disney, Walt, 209
Disraeli, Benjamin, 72
Dumbledore, Professor (*Harry Potter* character), 208
Dunst, Kirsten, 117
Dylan, Bob, 163

E.T. (*E.T.* character), 201
Edison, Thomas, 211
Einstein, Albert, 153
Eisenhower, Dwight D., 225
Eliot, George, 127, 200
Eliot, T. S., 177
Eloise (Kay Thompson's character), 20
Emerson, Ralph Waldo, 5, 33, 84, 93, 102, 247
Epictetus, 205

Faiz, Faiz Ahmed, 138
Fallon, Jimmy, 101
Feynman, Richard, 153
Field, Sally, 168
Fields, W. C., 43, 223, 236
Fitzgerald, Ella, 3
Fitzgerald, F. Scott, 228
Fitzgerald, Zelda, 129
Flaubert, Gustave, 233
Foer, Jonathan Safran, 207
Fonda, Jane, 34
France, Anatole, 231
Francis of Assisi, Saint, 4
Frank, Anne, 122, 161, 182

Franklin, Ben, 149, 232
Franzen, Jonathan, 12
Frasier, Walt "Clyde," 154
Frost, Robert, 234
Fuller, Thomas, 102, 151

Gandhi, Indira, 65
Gandhi, Mahatma, 173
Gandhi, Mohandas, 133
Garland, Judy, 10, 81
Gauguin, Paul, 120
Gelbart, Larry, 216
Gellar, Sarah Michelle, 57, 185
Gershwin, George, 137
Gibran, Kahlil, 115
Gielgud, John, Sir, 205
Gill, Elaine, 239
Giuliani, Rudy, 198
Goethe, Johann Wolfgang von, 11
Goldberg, Whoopi, 226
Golding, William, 48
Goldman, William, 236
Goodman, Allegra, 160
Goodwin, Joe, 51
Gould, Stephen Jay, 25
Goytisolo, Juan, 169
Grafton, Sue, 191
Graham, Katherine, 206
Graham, Martha, 69
Grant, Hugh, 136
Groening, Matt, 214
Gurney, A. R., 236

Hamilton, Jane, 89
Harris, Xander (*Buffy the Vampire Slayer* character), 166
Harrison, George, 57
Heaney, Seamus, 197
Heimel, Cynthia, 74

Hein, Piet, 148
Heine, Heinrick, 121
Hellman, Lillian, 108
Hemingway, Ernest, 221, 228, 235
Hepburn, Katharine, 12, 208
Heraclitus, 26
Hewitt, Jennifer Love, 139
Hill, Lauryn, 148
Hippocrates, 40
Høeg, Peter, 152
Holzer, Jenny, 232
Homer, 72
Hopkins, Anthony, 38
Horace, 85
Hughes, Langston, 186
Hughes, Sarah, 208
Huong, Ho Xuan, 136
Hurston, Zora Neale, 27, 153, 221, 236

Irving, John, 185

Jackson, Andrew, 23
Jackson, Janet, 185
Jeffrey, Robbie, 126
Jeffrey, Sarah, 126
Jian, Ma, 169
Johnson, Crockett, 219
Johnson, Lady Bird, 67
Johnson, Samuel, 65, 184
Jolie, Angelina, 37
Jones, Marion, 210
Jordan, Michael, 231
Juárez, Benito, 28

Karr, Mary, 11
Kato, Shidzue, 16
Keith, Kent M., 219
Keller, Helen, 4, 61
Kellum, Milton, 139

Kennedy, John F., 26
Kennedy, Robert F., 24
Kerr, Jean, 35
Keys, Alicia, 36, 152
Kidman, Nicole, 171
King, Martin Luther, Jr., 25, 90, 222
Kingsolver, Barbara, 198
Knowles, Beyoncé, 161
Konigsburg, E. L., 120
Krauss, Ruth, 219
Kudrow, Lisa, 73
Kushner, Tony, 27

Lachey, Nick, 165
Lamott, Anne, 216
L'Amour, Louis, 28
Lang, k.d., 138
Lao-Tse, 228
Lemons, Abe, 212
L'Engle, Madeleine, 216
Lennon, John, 14, 128, 182
Levine, Gail Carson, 82
Lewis, C. S., 66
Lin, Maya, 148
Lincoln, Abraham, 92, 137, 183
Lindbergh, Anne Morrow, 84, 160
Linus (Peanuts character), 28
Little, Mary Elizabeth Davidson, 143
Lombardi, Vince, 223, 224
Longfellow, Henry Wadsworth, 163
Longworth, Alice Roosevelt, 85
Lopez, Jennifer, 21, 45
Lopez, Nancy, 164
Lorde, Audre, 113, 147, 236
Love, Courtney, 57
Lowry, Lois, 66, 185

McCartney, Linda, 187
McCartney, Paul, 136, 187

McDermott, Dylan, 37
McLean, AJ, 81
McMillan, Terry, 187
Madonna, 217
Maimonides, 145
Malcolm X, 24, 143
Manheim, Camryn, 45
Márquez, Gabriel García, 160
Marshall, James, 209
Martin, Steve, 121
Marx, Groucho, 52, 135, 179
Mathison, Melissa, 201
Mauriac, François, 116
May, Stephanie, 126
Mays, Willie, 164
Meir, Golda, 233
Millay, Edna St. Vincent, 138
Milne, A A 197, 215
Mitchell, Joni, 85
Mitchell, Margaret, 39, 150
Molière, 3
Montaigne, Michel de, 22, 248
Moore, Lorrie, 100
Morley, Christopher, 68, 218, 224
Morrison, Toni, 68
Moses, Grandma, 222
Moss, Kate, 45
Munro, H. H., 193
Musset, Alfred de, 121

Nash, Ogden, 226
Nevelson, Louise, 234
Nin, Anaïs, 22, 232
Norman, Jessye, 234

Oakley, Annie, 234
Oates, Joyce Carol, 20
O'Brien, Conan, 109
O'Brien, Edna, 104

O'Connor, Sandra Day, 211
O'Donnell, Rosie, 119
O'Farrell, John, 181
O'Hara, Scarlett (*Gone With the Wind* character),
    150
O'Keeffe, Georgia, 171
Olivier, Laurence, Sir, 220
Olmos, Edward James, 26
Orwell, George, 159
Osment, Haley Joel, 146
Otis, Carré, 53
Owens, Jesse, 235

Paderewski, Ignacy, 216
Paltrow, Gwyneth, 37
Parker, Dorothy, 21
Parry, James, 77
Pascal, Blaise, 85, 221
Peter, Lawrence J., 18
Peter Pan (*Peter Pan* character), 74
Picasso, Pablo, 25, 99, 150, 171
Pinter, Harold, 162
Plutarch, 113
Porter, Cole, 120
Portman, Natalie, 170
Powell, Colin, 123
Prinze, Freddie, Jr., 12, 211
Proust, Marcel, 78
Proverbs
    Chinese, 34, 111, 181, 210, 219
    Czech, 87
    Flemish, 88
    Italian, 85
    Irish, 22
    Polish, 109
    Turkish, 79
Pym, Barbara, 188

Quindlen, Anna, 17, 173, 205, 213

Quixote, Don (*Don Quixote* character), 109

Rafiki (*The Lion King* character), 192
Rather, Dan, 73
Rhea, Caroline, 24, 123
Ricci, Christina, 60
Richards, Ann, 19
Rick (*Casablanca* character), 95
Rivers, Joan, 122
Roberts, Julia, 3, 13, 35, 115
Rochefoucauld, François de la, 99, 196, 232
Rock, Chris, 3
Rockwell, Norman, 53
Roosevelt, Eleanor, 78, 91
Roseanne, 44
Rowland, Kelly, 89
Rowling, J. K., 144, 178, 208
Rubinstein, Arthur, 15
Rudolph, Wilma, 183
Russo, Richard, 177

Sacker, Ira, 46
Safire, William, 158
Sanskrit (poem), 16
Sarandon, Susan, 169
Schulz, Charles, 28, 103
Schwarzenegger, Arnold, 223
Scott, Walter, Sir, 22
Sendak, Maurice, 30
Seuss, Dr., 236
Shakespeare, William, 66, 75, 94, 99, 122, 132, 145, 172
Shaw, Artie, 163
Shaw, George Bernard, 42, 68, 71, 76, 129, 218, 226, 233
Shawn, Wallace, 11
Shay, Larry, 51
Shear, Claudia, 80
Shields, Carol, 201

Sills, Beverly, 212
Simpson, Bart (*The Simpsons* character), 19
Simpson, Homer (*The Simpsons* character), 157, 214
Simpson, Marge (*The Simpsons* character), 214
Sinatra, Frank, 139
Sitwell, Edith, 38
Snyder, Principal (*Buffy the Vampire Slayer* character), 59
Solzhenitsyn, Aleksandr, 26
Sorvino, Mira, 44
Spears, Britney, 67
Spielberg, Stephen, 201
Stegner, Wallace, 232
Stein, Gertrude, 30, 228
Steinbeck, John, 47, inside back cover
Steinem, Gloria, 3, 26
Stevenson, Robert Louis, 66, 235
Stoppard, Tom, 127
Streisand, Barbra, 29
Sturges, Preston, 87, 233
Styron, William, 154
Swift, Jonathan, 121
Symborska, Wislawa, 198
Syrus, Publius, 5

Temple, Shirley, 17
Tennyson, Lord, Alfred, 4, 121
Teresa, Mother, 177, 195
Thompson, Kay, 20
Thoreau, Henry David, 19, 118
Thurber, James, 28, 58, 228
Timberlake, Justin, 123, 126
Tolstoy, Leo, 100, 106, 134
Tomlin, Lily, 83
Travers, P. L., 117
Trollope, Anthony, 14
Tubman, Harriet, 235

Twain, Mark, 43, 54, 62, 70, 76, 113, 154,
   190, 234

Vess, Tabitha, 167
Vinci, Leonardo da, 161
Viorst, Judith, 179
Voltaire, 21
Vonnegut, Kurt, inside back cover
Vreeland, Diana, 35

Wagner, Jane, 70
Walker, Alice, 189
Washington, Booker T., 89, 191
Washington, Denzel, 22
Washington, George, 78
Waugh, Evelyn, 76
Wayne, John, 22
Webb, Emily (*Our Town* character), 16
Welles, Orson, 42
Welty, Eudora, 24, 206
Whitehead, Alfred North, 155
Whitman, Walt, 33, 128
Whittier, John Greenleaf, 102
Wicked Witch of the West (*The Wizard of Oz*
   character), 192
Wilcox, Ella Wheeler, 114, 189
Wilde, Oscar, 134, 233
Wilder, Billy, 209
Wilder, Laura Ingalls, 232
Wilder, Thornton, 16
Williams, Serena, 189
Williams, Tennessee, 15, 136, 227
Winfrey, Oprah, 91, 191, 207, 235
Witherspoon, Reese, 72
Wonder, Stevie, 61
Woods, Tiger, 56
Woolf, Virginia, 110, 189

Yogananda, Paramahansa, 120

Young, Neil, 57
Youngman, Henny, 36

Zellweger, Renée, 40
Zola, Émile, 233

acknowledgments

Tis the good reader that makes the good book.

−ralph waldo emerson

Thank *you* for reading this book!

I also want to thank my wonderful editor and friend, Elise Howard. I am proud and grateful to have written three books for her. Thanks, too, to editor Tui Sutherland, careful and caring shepherd who nudged these pages all the way to publication. My agent, Laura Peterson, and editor Jennifer Weiss also provided advice and encouragement from the start.

My family deserves an enormous bouquet of thanks. My teen daughter Elizabeth Ackerman found tons of quotes, sometimes on demand. ("Lizzi, look for one from Alicia Keys.") My daughter Emme offered the point of view of a sage preteen. My husband Robert, bless him, has probably read more advice for teens over the years than any man alive. My mother, Marybeth Weston Lobdell; brother Mark Weston; sister-in-law, Cynthia Weston; stepsister Ali Lobdell; nephew Scott Lobdell, and Aunt Diana Bird, all gave helpful notes for this book, as did Matt Bird, Anna Ausubel, Stephanie May, and the Squam Lake Cousins! My niece, Sarah Jeffrey, read the manuscript cover to cover and returned it with questions, comments, and funny doodles.

I even leaned on teen neighbors: Daniel Wilcox, James Anthony, and Peter Bumcrot (who read with guys' eyes), and Louisa Strauss, Mathilda McGee-Tubb, and Stephanie Jenkins (whose scribbles were invaluable).

Maureen Davison went beyond the call of friendship and gave a thorough and thoughtful reading to two chapters.

Yale students Sophie Raseman, Colleen Kinder, Danielle Tumminio, and Kelly McGannon all separately dedicated vacation days to the *For Teens Only* cause. I am grateful to them and impressed by them.

Thank you, Nancy Sander, Lauren Westbrook, and Matty Reategui for providing quiet days.

And finally, here's to the eloquent men and women who spoke so quotably, and the journalists who first collected their words. As Michel de Montaigne wrote, "I have gathered a posie of other people's flowers, and nothing but the thread that binds them is my own."

Always say thank you.

Don't miss this great read!

A SHORT BOOK THAT'S LONG ON ADVICE!

For Girls Only can help you know yourself, get along better with friends and family, understand guys, excel in school, realize your ambitions, and become a more confident person.

Includes over four hundred carefully chosen quotations from around the world and throughout time!

Available wherever books are sold.

An *Imprint of* HarperCollins*Publishers*

www.harperchildrens.com • www.carolweston.com